TAKE BACK YOUR HEALTH

- Clean up and detoxify the body

- Revitalize your organs and brain functioning at the cellular level

- Intuit for Yourself What You Should Do Each Day for Your Health

BY MEDICAL INTUITIVE SCOTT WERNER, MD

BALBOA.
PRESS

A DIVISION OF HAY HOUSE

Balboa Press books may be ordered through booksellers or by contacting:

Balboa Press
A Division of Hay House
1663 Liberty Drive
Bloomington, IN 47403
www.balboapress.com
1-(877) 407-4847

Because of the dynamic nature of the Internet, any web addresses or links contained in this book may have changed since publication and may no longer be valid. The views expressed in this work are solely those of the author and do not necessarily reflect the views of the publisher, and the publisher hereby disclaims any responsibility for them.

The author of this book does not dispense medical advice or prescribe the use of any technique as a form of treatment for physical, emotional, or medical problems without the advice of a physician, either directly or indirectly. The intent of the author is only to offer information of a general nature to help you in your quest for emotional and spiritual well-being. In the event you use any of the information in this book for yourself, which is your constitutional right, the author and the publisher assume no responsibility for your actions.

Any people depicted in stock imagery provided by Thinkstock are models, and such images are being used for illustrative purposes only. Certain stock imagery © Thinkstock.

Printed in the United States of America

ISBN: 978-1-4525-6289-6 (e)
ISBN: 978-1-4525-6288-9 (sc)
ISBN: 978-1-4525-6290-2 (hc)
Library of Congress Control Number: 2012921245
Balboa Press rev. date:11/09/2012

TABLE OF CONTENTS

Introduction:

Take Back Your Health is written with the intent to empower each individual to take back control of your own body and health. Over the past thirty years, I have assisted thousands of people through my knowledge of Medicine, physiology, anatomy, herbology, homeopathic remedies, essential oils, and now energetics.

This book has been created from channeling Angels and guides, with the Blessing of the higher beings of light and Master Healers, to assist the beings of Earth in healing their physical bodies, release toxic buildup, and restore functioning to organs and systems of the body. The book will also balance your emotional, mental, and spiritual body, and align your biomeridians.

The book itself vibrates in unconditional Love. The energy and knowledge of this book will transform your life as the energy and knowledge is transmuted to you and your Loved ones.

Do not read this book cover to cover unless you want knowledge.

Each page is designed to give a personal intuitive reading of what you should do today, for a few days, or a month or the next few months, or for the rest of your life.

The choice is yours. To be "Sick and Tired" or "Healthy, Strong and Happy". Basic Instructions will be on each page and you will be guided in your own intuitive reading. If more information is required, you may call Dr. Werner and make an appointment for a more in depth Medical Intuitive Spiritual reading at 435-986-0025. You may also see a healer, homeopathic, Naturopathic, or Chiropractic physician of your choice to further your knowledge and healing. Many souls have come to Earth at this time to help and assist your evolution.

This book was written for you. The book will empower you, revitalize you, instruct you and give you ideas and herbal regimes to benefit your health. Your own soul will direct your hands to the page you need to find help, encouragement, cleansing, rebalancing, removing energetic blockages, and much more.

So now you're ready to get started. Tell your hands to open the book with the intent to *Take Back Your Health*. Then just open the book to where your soul desires for you to begin

But if you're not ready, put the book under your pillow or on your nightstand. Simply by being in your energetic field, the book's energy will assist you. If you're totally not ready, let someone you Love use the book.

May the Universe Bless you with Devine Love, prosperity and health.

Exercise, Exercise, Exercise

Today I will start to exercise, do an outdoor or indoor sport, go for a walk, and get my body moving. (I told you not to just read the book!)

Benefits of exercise:

Do you want to feel better, have more energy and perhaps even live longer? Look no further than exercise. The health benefits of regular exercise and physical activity are hard to ignore. And the benefits of exercise are yours for the taking, regardless of your age, sex, or physical ability.

Exercise controls weight

Exercise can help prevent excess weight gain or help maintain weight loss. When you engage in physical activity, you burn calories.

Exercise controls disease

Regular physical activity can help you prevent or manage a wide range of health problems and concerns, including; poor circulation, hypertension, heart disease, stroke, metabolic syndrome, type 2 diabetes, depression, and certain types of cancer, arthritis, and falls.

Exercise helps with Depression, Mood Disorders, and Stress

Go workout at the gym, play tennis or take a 30-minute walk. Physical activity stimulates various brain chemicals and hormones that can leave you feeling happier and more relaxed. You may also feel better about your appearance when you exercise regularly, which can boost your confidence and improve your self-esteem

Exercise boosts energy

Regular physical activity can improve your muscle strength and boost your endurance. Exercise and physical activity deliver oxygen and nutrients to your tissues and help your cardiovascular system work more efficiently. When your heart and lungs work more efficiently, you have more energy to go about your daily chores. Exercise can also enhance circulation to the glands which improves the hormones in men and women. Cellular health is also stimulated with exercise.

Exercise helps you sleep better

Regular physical activity can help you fall asleep faster and deepen your sleep. If you exercise too close to bedtime, may get yourself too energized to fall asleep, so program your exercise at least three hours prior to your bedtime.

Story time:

A women who I treated, had fibromyalgia/chronic fatigue syndrome. When she first developed this disease, an emotional trauma was energetically incorporated into every cell of her body, causing her entire body to ache. Exercise and movement made the pain even worse. She would lie in bed each day in pain.

During this era of medicine, no one really believed she had a disease. Most doctors felt it was psychological. SSRI medications, the first of which was Prozac, had just been marketed, and were being used for psychological illness. Antidepressants did help with the emotional trauma and somewhat by numbing her mind. All of the medical technological studies and laboratory testing which were done on her physical body demonstrated there was nothing really wrong. Many of the doctors felt she was malingering (making up symptoms to get attention).

As I watched her disease progress, she gained weight from inactivity and from treating herself with "comfort foods" because of the pain and mental anguish she was going through. My intuition told me something really was physically wrong. My intuition further told me, emotions had caused her disease, but energy blockages and viruses had entered her body during the whole process. I knew that lying in bed would only worsen her circulation and her symptoms.

When her doctors continually received complaints of the symptoms of pain, they first tried anti-inflammatory pharmaceuticals, which caused severe stomach upset and worsened kidney and liver function. They then went to steroids to decrease the inflammation. The steroids made her rapidly gain weight, but they did alleviate some of the symptoms which made her feel better. So despite the weight gain, they continued the steroids. After she had gained over 100 pounds, the doctors realizeed, steroids were not the answer. So to control the pain, they started her on narcotics. At first, just a few Lortab each day. This would control the pain for a few hours, but left her feeling lifeless as the drugs wore off. There was also increased pain between dosages. Stronger doses were prescribed, needed and used, and eventually higher doses of stronger narcotics were needed and used to control the pain.

I knew this was a cycle that needed to stop.

I started a search, which led me first to magnetic pads, magnetic mattresses, magnetic foot inserts. These all helped to decrease the pain to a certain degree. Then I started anti-inflammatory herbs, and antiviral homeopathic remedies, both of which helped tremendously. The pain medicines were continued by the medical doctors, which caused additional problems of constipation and bowel difficulties. Candida, a type of fungus, infected her body and started to cause crepitance (air bubbles) in joints and connective tissues. Intuitively, I knew something more needed to be done. With the weight gain, exercise was difficult. She did get up and move around, but would often end up in bed, taking more pain medicine. She had deep seated emotions of anger, shame, regret, blame, and guilt.

As we worked to release these emotions, she started to improve, moving around and started walking. Anti-inflammatory herbs helped her by reducing the inflammation and anti-viral herbal combinations helped decrease the viral load. Antifungal herbs reduced the Candida and other fungus, helping to rid her body of the aflotoxins produced by the fungus. As her ability to exercise increased, endorphins and enkephalins levels increased in her body, reducing her pain and inflammation. Continued reduction in her emotional component through alternative psychological therapies helped her deal with life issues. Introduction of herbal pain remedies to control her opioid addiction, reduced her need for these addictive substances. It took several years, many healers and many healing modalities, but today she is totally functional and off all medication.

TODAY I BLESS THE WATER I DRINK AND I DRINK 8 TALL GLASSES TODAY AND EVERY DAY

Water is the most abundant complex molecule in your body, Science is still discovering the healing complexity and simplicity of water.

Water can be changed by our intent and blessing.

Water helps to detox the body.

Dr. Masura Emoto of Japan did multiple studies of the effects of blessing water and putting words on water-filled containers. By freezing the water, he was able to show the effects of words and blessings on the crystallization process.

Water holds vibration and intent. To create healing from water, fill a closable container with water. Gently shake it, tap it in the palm of your hand, gently with the intent to energize and bless the water for your body. This is called potentizing.

A lady recently came into the office to sell Chinese water bottles. It had a filter, magnets, minerals, and a device to improve the water, but required the person to shake it, to infuse energy. Just the belief and the action of intent does change the water for purposes of creating health.

Alkalizing water can also be beneficial. Start by adding ¼ tsp real salt, Himalayan salt or sea salt to a pint of water. Adding the mineral salts, helps raise the pH of the water making it better for your body. You don't need to go out and buy an Alkalizing water device, unless you want the energy of your money to flow out.

Story Time:

My wife was preparing to run the St. George Marathon. I would be running with her to give her encouragement. There was a fountain at a park about three miles into the run, but the water tasted awful. I decided to practice what I preach, so I blessed the water to taste good and to be good for everyone who would drink it. To this day, I Love the taste of that fountain. My whole family laughs about this, because when they drank from the fountain, it tasted so good.

TODAY I BLESS MY FOOD, AND EVERYTHING I TAKE INTO MY BODY

Blessing my food puts energy into the food. It raises the vibration of the food. It transmutes the molecular structure to make it more compatible with my digestive system and the cells throughout the body.

By blessing my food, I create the intention to remove and disables toxins or chemicals, transmute and disable negative emotional energy, which may be in the food. Over the years, human beings have created thousands of chemicals, toxins and compounds, which can suppress and damage the immune system. These chemicals are in everything. We created these substances, and we can un-create them with our intent and thoughts.

Modern corporations with their emphasis on mass production and profits attempted to improve the quality and quantity of food. Perhaps the intentions were good in the beginning, but I won't go into the details of what happened, except that profit, control and greed has changed the food supply and distribution.

Fortunately, expressing gratitude to the plants and animals and thanking them for feeding us and blessing our bodies with health, can change and maximise the energy of food.

Story time:

My wife Vicki and I had just read an eye opening book about being skinny, and watched a movie about food production and the quality of our food. Vicki made the decision to become vegetarian. A year earlier, we had decided to raise our own chickens for the eggs and to have chickens on a farm that also has cattle. While I was taking care of the chickens one evening, Vicki was communicating with the cattle, sending them Love, telling them how sorry she felt for their plight. The cattle spoke to her mind and said, "We Love you. We came into this existence knowing we would be killed to feed people, and we are grateful to sacrifice ourselves for that purpose".

Plants, animals, and all of the elements of this Earth are here for us and our use. We need to express gratitude and thankfulness for their desire and Love for us, and to bless them with our Love for them.

Second Story Time:

Traveling through Peru two years ago, I Blessed, and sent Love to all the water I drank and food I ate. Vicki and I ate the same foods and water, but Vicki came down with "Tourista", that is,E. coli, a very painful form of dysentery, (Stomach pain with diarrhea) As I look back on why I didn't also get sick, sure I'm larger, (weigh more) and eat stuff off the ground, but there may have been a difference in energy and intention.

I went to Peru to immerse myself in the culture, believing I could eat, drink, and live the life of that country, blessing everything with Love and goodness. I even drank from the spring waters coming from ancient sources and was scolded for doing so.

Vicki started out with thought's of, "I hope I don't get sick from the food" "I need to be careful of the water, fruits, salads and vegetables." Those thoughts might have created a weakness in her system, letting the bugs get anchored, causing bowel problems.

TODAY I AM GRATEFUL FOR AND BLESS MY BODY TO FUNCTION PERFECTLY AND BE HEALED

Gratitude definition: thankfulness, gratefulness, or appreciation is a feeling, an energy, emotion or attitude in acknowledgment of a benefit that one has received or will receive.

When I have an "Attitude of Gratitude", the energy enters into my cellular matrix, which produces a higher spiritual vibration, which by itself will start the healing process.

Gratitude can make me happy.

Thanking others can make them happy.

Being grateful reminds me of the good things in my life and what is important.

Gratitude can turn bad things into good things.

Be grateful to be alive, look at the alternative.

If life brings challenges, gratitude helps give me purpose, giving me strength to overcome.

Gratitude helps me have purpose.

Story Time:

I spent time as a missionary in Puerto Rico. A local saying was: "Si Tengo mi Salud, tengo todo". Rough translation, "If I have my health, I have everything". Onc time, I was having a bad day; we had just had a family turn us away, so my missionary companion and I were riding our bikes down a highway when a speeding car hit me on my bike, throwing me into a telephone pole. I woke up with a sheet over my face, hearing some women speaking in Spanish. They said, "What strange underwear these Americans wear," and "How sad that such a young man died." I tore the sheet off my head and sat up. Needless to say the nurses screamed: "Aye dios mio!." They started saying how grateful they were that I was alive. Apparently, I had been declared dead and was waiting to be taken to the morgue. Since that experience, I've always be grateful to be alive. I also owe to that experience, coming back knowing my purpose in life, which is; to help others find health and their life purpose. Find a way to be grateful for your experiences, for they are lessons to teach you, and can become your greatest blessings.

Today I Bless and I am Grateful for My Family and Close Relationships

Each of us come to the earth to learn different aspects of unconditional Love.

This is the concept that I should Love and be grateful for the people who are my greatest teachers.

This includes, my parents, my gandparents, siblings, spouses and children.

Today, I will call them, tell them how grateful I am for them.

I will remind them of some special experience we shared, and express gratitude for that experience. I will tell them how much I care about them and express my Love for them.

I will call my spouse, significant other, or a good friend, and express my Love for them.

If there are family members from whom I have become distanced, I will call them today, I will tell them, I miss them and their friendship, tell them I am sorry and ask for their forgiveness. I will tell them how grateful I am for being in the same family. I will appreciate their friendship and the lessons I have learned from them.

Story Time:

My grandmother, June Nichols, died while I was in Medical school. She has fallen, breaking her hip, and shortly after, fatty emboli from the injured tissue, shot into her lungs, so she couldn't breathe. She died from suffication.

My mother didn't tell me about her dying and I missed the funeral. I always felt bad about this, so I used a technique, calling in June Nichol's over soul to discuss this with her. It turned out to be such a healing experience for both of us. It actually helped her to go back to source energy, to evolve, as she had been stuck earthbound without moving into the Light to get processed on the other side. And it helped me get over the guilt of not attending her funeral. (Guilt is a very low vibration) This connection with my grandmother, helped my vibration to improve and improved my ability to heal others -- including myself.

2nd Story Time:

When I was practicing medicine, I had a marvelous nurse practitioner who worked with me at the office. When I closed down the office, he was disappointed and angry, and started a lawsuit against me. The feelings and tension which came from this lawsuit almost destroyed the relationship.

I wrote him a letter expressing my Love and appreciation for him, and told him that I was sorry about our professional and personal relationship ending. I asked for his

Forgiveness, told him how grateful I was to be his friend and how I enjoyed working with him all the years we were together. He responded very favorably and forgave me, opening up to a renewed friendship.

Today is the Day to Spend Time to Heal a Relationship with a Spouse, Significant Other, Parent, Sibling, or Friend

Sometimes those whom I should hold nearest and dearest to my heart, have wronged me, or I have pushed them away and out of my life.

Today, I will spend some time on the phone healing that relationship, or will talk with them in person, or connect with their higher-self.

Practice:

Communicating with the higher self may be a new concept for you.

Begin by taking a deep breath, intent to clear your energy, to enter your higher-self, (where soul is connected to source). Then breathe again, focusing your thoughts with intent to call in the higher-self of whomever you want to communicate with on a soul level. Call them by name. Ask their permission to communicate. You might say, "May I talk with the higher soul of [their name]? You will "feel" a yes or a no. If yes is the answer, start speaking with your heart open, full of Love and compassion, healing the relationship as you go. Listen with your heart. Feel the emotions and Love of their soul. Thank them for communicating with you, Ask forgiveness if necessary. Express Love and gratitude. Then close with thankfulness and unconditional Love for their being.

If the answer was "No" seek out a spiritual healer with greater knowledge to help with healing the soul connection.

Story Time:

When I was a child, my older brother and I didn't get along. He would break something, and blame it on me. He and his friends would make fun of me, causing me heart ache and loneliness.

We drifted apart as time went on. As a grown man, I was angry inside, because of my childhood being tough, because of him. I know this anger was causing some of my health problems.

Because of my brothers own health problems, communuicating directly with him had been impossible. '

One night, the heaviness was getting to me, so I breathed deeply, clearing my thoughts. I then called in my higher-self, my connection to source. I then called in my brothers' higher self with intent to communicate my Love for him and ask for a resolution to this issue. His higher self communicated to me with Love and compassion. His energy told me, he had never intended to cause me grief or heart ache. It was my perception of the situations, taking the blame and guilt which produced my anger. He was just having fun with his friends, and they didn't want the "little brother" hanging out with them. When I had taken the blame for breaking things, he, at the time didn't realize, I would be beaten. He felt the parents would be kinder to me because I was little. He had always felt guilty and had hoped someday, I would forgive him.

As I closed this spiritual communication, I had renewed Love for my brother. It has helped me to visit him, and Love him more in this life.

TODAY I SPEND TIME WITH SOMEONE I LOVE

Family members or friends who have healthy relationships spend time with one another.

Indeed, family time or friend time is a fundamental building block to strengthening bonds.

Families or friends who share meal times and take the time to discuss activities often have better opportunities for establishing healthy relationships.

Family members or friends can spend time together one-on-one in addition to time spent as a group with all family members or friends present.

Story Time:

In my first marriage, my wife didn't like my family. Even at Christmas, we would visit only long enough to get the presents. My children from that marriage never got to know my parents. Twenty three years later, I am divorced, remarried, and now have two more children. We now spend more time at my parents house. The children feel comfortable at their house and my parents started inviting us to more activities. They even invited us to go on a trip with them, renting a condominium for a week, so we could stay close to them. My first five children feel very uncomfortable at my parent's house to this day. They never really got to know them.

Part of healing, is working out relationship problems as best we can.

If distance is a problem or just getting together doesn't work, go into your higher self and call in the person you're having trouble with or just want to contact. Tell them you Love them, you're grateful for them, you're sorry not to be able to spend more time with them. Forgive them, and ask for their forgiveness. Then the relationship can heal both of you

HEALTHY COMMUNICATION TODAY
WITH MYSELF AND OTHERS

Healthy relationships exhibit characteristics of good communication. Words are things!

Today, I will communicate in a positive way with myself and others, and check the words and energy I am expressing.

Self talk, or how I mentally "speak to myself" can affect my health and create energy which affects us on a cellular level: "as a man thinketh, so he is."

My friend Katherine Beck, psychic, mentor, teacher, taught the universe gives us 20-30 seconds before a statement or a thought starts to incorporate it into our cellular matrix and bodies. (Spiritual, Mental, Emotional, Physical)

Katherine taught, When I make a negative statement or thought, as soon as recognize it, I say out loud, 'I cancel [the negative emotion or statement]'

Then, "I replace [the negative emotion or statement] with [the opposite positive emotion or statement]," This cancels the energy of the negative thoughts or statements and keeps it from incorporating into the cells of the body.

Words are things, energy, greatly positive or negative

During meal times, there will be positive or negative conversations, within the group.

Positive discussions, instead of silence, or negative conversation can be both emotionally stimulating, and be physically beneficial to digestion, and set the tone for the entire evening. Happy and joyfull conversation is the best medicine.

Positive ideas exchanged with families or friends with good communication skills is healing.

Family members or friends can express their emotions, fears and desires without dread/fear of repercussion, when unconditional Love and non-judgment is present.

It is my job to infuse Love and laughter into conversations.

Families will periodically undergo times of conflict, and healthy families exhibit the ability to communicate and work through any conflict with Love, Forgiveness and positive thoughts.

Storytime:

For years, in my previous marriage, the family would get together every Sunday at the parents of my ex-spouse, and discuss problematic people in the family. It was never a discussion with love and with insight, but a constant harassment and 'roast" of these individuals. And if you were not present for the conversation, they would speak ill of you.

Because of the negative energy expressed, I would feel uncomfortable with the conversation, and I always felt like defending the individual in question. As I look back at this now, I realize it was tearing the family apart.

I would attempt to defend the person or family in question. Then they would start on how I wasn't doing everything I should be doing.

Think how great it can be for a family to get together and just express positive thoughts and stories. That energy will carry into the night and into the dreams and thoughts of those present. It would set the stage for a better day tomorrow.

TODAY I WILL TRUST MYSELF
AND THE UNIVERSE

Health and Healthy relationships go hand in hand. In order to have health, I will trust my decisions to do the right things, eat the right food, say positive words, think positive thoughts, about myself and others.

I will trust that the universal source energy (i.e. God energy) will take care of me and help give me the correct information to guide me on my path.

Angel's will assist and protect me, on my path, and direct me to fulfill my life's purpose.

As a family member or friend, I will trust that the universe will assist me in my relationships.

Trust can be a critical characteristic for parents and children. Parents can be overprotective and feel a need to be hovering around their children during most non-school hours. Healthy parental

relationships exhibit a trust that the children feel, infusing energy into the child to make correct decisions, based on family values that the parents have instilled.

Today I will trust myself to make good decisions, and trust that the universe will assist me.

Story Time:

My wife, always makes very clear what she expects of our children. She never leaves them wondering what they should or should not do. Whenever they are left with a grandparent or someone more liberal, they always say, "my Mother wouldn't want me to do that" or "This isn't healthy for me". They trust their Mother and Father because we are stable in our thoughts and actions. We have taught our children what behavior is expected. Then, we trust them!

Many people who are self destructive, never develop trust in themselves to do the right thing. When a choice presents itself, in which you are unsure if it will harm you or someone else, ask for guidance. Ask the Angels to help you choose wisely, then trust your guidance. Move forward with faith and trust in yourself. Avoiding choices, causes stagnation, stops the flow of energy, hurting us spiritually and physically.

The universe provides for us and will give you what you desire.

Trust yourself and others. This energy and this thought will help you both do the right thing.

I CALL THE MASTER HEALERS AND BEINGS OF LIGHT TO ASSIST MY HEALING

This is a powerful way to heal myself, restore perfection to my body, emotions, and soul. I do this with people all the time, and do it unconsciously (but with the right intent) for health.

I take a deep breath, with the intent to clear my body and thoughts. I Hold the breath for 10 seconds. When releasing the breath, I do so with the intent to release what's bothering me right now.

I take another breath and hold for 10 seconds, with the intent to call the Master healers (Jesus, Buddha, Lao Tsu, Tsu Long and others) in whom I have Faith, with the intent to receive Healing.

I release the breath visualizing the Master Healers assisting me with Love and with light infusing my body, my emotions and my thoughts.

If there is a specific concern -- for example, an organ or tissue needing surgical intervention, I ask the surgical healers to assist me, and give them permission to intervene.

I Send the Healers, Love and Gratitude for taking care of me. When they are done, I thank them for their assistance and I am open to follow-up visits as needed.

I use this technique as often as needed.

Storytime:

Vicki and I were considering a trip to Brazil, to meet John of God, and to see how people there are healed and to be healed. Vicki's Mom loaned us the book about John of God, by Heather Cumming and Karen Leffler, and as we read, it revealed how John heals the people. John of God's Faith opens the heavens and channels the energy necessary for those who come to him to heal. But there is more. Various Master healing beings and crossed over surgeons, with marvelous skills for healing, assist him. As the Faith required for the people desiring to heal is proven and matured, with their belief and faith being so deep, they can allow John to cut anywhere on the body, -- even their eye with a blunt kitchen knife or other instrument, trusting him with their life. These healers are here for all, to call upon.

In November of 2011, a knife like pain started stabbing me just below my stomach with swelling after every meal. Intuitively I asked what was causing the pain. "Your pancreas," said the Masters. The pain was worsening by the hour. I was unsure what to do. As we had been reading about John of God, I wondered if I could go to Brazil to be healed. As the pain worsened I knew I wouldn't be able to travel much longer. That night, I called upon the Masters of Healing, as well as John of God and his inspired healers. I awoke the next morning feeling as if I was coming out of anesthesia. I felt as if there had been many healers in the room that night healing my body and organs and doing spiritual surgery on my system. I knew that my prayers had been answered.

Today is the day I call upon the Master Healers to heal me.
Faith is the Key! Asking is the Action. Healing is the result.

Additional Story Time:

This is a powerful story going along with this concept.

On the second day of writing this book in February 2012, I decided to hike up a hill near where I was staying in Hawaii. The couple I was staying with said, "to go up to the end of this main road till it ends, park the car and hike up the trail." At the end of the road there was a sign saying "No Parking". So I turned the car around heading down the hill, parked the car about twenty yards down in front of a house. (Thought I was in the parking zone)

I hiked the trail to the top. It was a magical view, of mountains with clouds, a rainbow, with rain coming from the north and east, the glistening Pacific Ocean to the south and Diamond Head majestically rising from the waters to the west. With the sun warming my back and chest, I felt so strong, no pain in any part of my body, heart and lungs functioning perfectly. The sun was beginning to set, so I started running back down the mountain with gratitude, I was feeling so good, just being in paradise.

When I arrived to the car, I caught the flash of a yellow paper under the windshield wiper. To my horror, I had a parking ticket on my rental car. Needless to say, I went into a not so high vibration and emotions, wondering why the police had come just when I was having such a wonderful time. I'm here to help everyone, doesn't he understand. "I hate police"

The second I made that statement, I knew I was in trouble. I noticed my right upper pre-molar (tooth), which is connected to the liver energetically, was starting to ache. I calmed down immediately knowing that my rage, my anger and my frustration were causing this pain to manifest into the physical. I hurriedly canceled the emotions, replacing them with peace, calm and forgiveness, knowing they were causing changes at a cellular level. But I was too slow. Pain entered into my cells.

I was hungry, so I removed the ticket from the windshield, found myself going into the anger/rage again. As I looked for several minutes for someplace to eat, without canceling out my negative emotions, the pain moved deeper into my tissues, then into my bones. Worse, the pain penetrated the maxilla and temporal bones of the right side of my face and skull, which started to throb. I felt my right upper abdomen spasm, with nausea spreading through my stomach, gallbladder and liver. I kept breathing deep meditative breaths to remove the pain and nausea which continued to worsen over the next four hours. I worsened to the point, I couldn't eat, deep nauseating pain spreading into my pancreas, where lies the sweetness in life. Dumbfounded at how fast I could go from pure ecstasy to misery I headed back to the bed and breakfast, where I was staying.

I lay down in bed, energy exhausted, wondering how I could find a dentist in the morning. Who I should call? How much it would cost? A lot more than the $35.00 parking ticket.

As I writhed in pain focusing on the negative, the thought came to me, "I'm supposed to be writing these fantastic books which will help people heal." "What is wrong with this situation?"

So, I began to think positively, thanking the police officer for doing his job. I asked the universe, "What purpose and message was I missing, not receiving, because the answers come so easily to me for others."

Then, an aha moment, I got it.

I thought of "Ho'oponopono" (a Hawaiian healing method) the police officer. I began sending Love to the police officer, saying I was sorry for being so angry. I asked him to forgive me for my rage and anger, forgiving and thanking him for protecting and serving the people. Then something magical happened. I asked in Faith (--believing and knowing they would come), for Jesus, the Master Healers, the Master Dentists and surgeons, John of God and his healers to come and heal me!By now, it was about 3 AM in the morning, I felt this energy of Love and Peace enfold my soul, surrounding and holding me. The Love brought me to tears. I felt the energy of the Masters and other beings of Light, take away my pain, and I fell into a deep sleep. I awoke at seven in the morning, feeling that I had been transformed. There was no pain, just pure, profound Gratitude and unconditional Love. And another story of a miracle. Thank you, officer!!!

TODAY I SET MY FOCAL POINT.

What is a focal point? A focal point is an objective or end result of what you set your intention and attention on. For example, usually when we desire to heal from a disease or an emotional process, we find someone who we believe knows more about it than us.

My daughter recently had a breast nodule and was sent by her family practice doctor, to an OB/GYN specialist, who sent her to a surgical specialist, who told her to monitor her condition for twelve weeks, start taking vitamin E., cut out caffeine, and start drinking green tea decaf.

But, she still has the breast cyst, and despite going from one person to another, she has still not got any resolution.

Many times we have emotional and physical issues and go from practitioner to practitioner thinking the issue has been resolved and yet it keeps popping back up.

We go from point A, to point B., to point C., to point D., to point E, to point F., to point G, etc. Thus, this new concept is to begin focusing on the issue at hand focusing on your focal point of the end result. You go from point A to point G. and skip the other steps.

It's easy to lose focus on what you really want and need when you're going from point A to point B to point C with a bunch of different authority figures. So the concept of setting a focal point means keeping your attention and intention focused on the end result. True, in the process of getting there many different steps may have to be taken, but mentally you always go from point A to the Focal Point and don't get distracted by the steps in between.

Storytime:

I had a severe infection which set into my thumb, began when I was picking weeds, and was stuck by a thorn into the center of my thumb. It started to fester, pyogenic bacteria, which are bacteria from the ground that degenerate living material into basic amino acids, minerals, and matter, that can be ingested by the plants.

With the thorn, in my thumb, the infection set in for about two weeks, and starting getting more painful. So good surgeon that I am, I started digging to get the thorn out. As I got deeper and deeper into the tissues and I finally retrieved what appeared to be a triangular piece of glass.

That night my thumb was very painful, and started to throb. It was swollen to three times the size of my other thumb. Since the swelling was my right thumb, right over the pineal point, I knew that energetically someone or something was getting to me through my celestial chakra.

So I prayed to know what was causing the problem energetically. I found through my prayers that there were four beings, who were sucking out my energy. I was giving energy to them and they had become energetic vampires. This was making me very sick. The infection worsened day by day. I wasn't sleeping due to the pain and I couldn't get my work done during the day.

The infection got so bad that the pus had to be removed. Again, I lanced my thumb, and pus did come out. However, that night the infection started spreading up into my blood vessels and joints of my thumb and wrist. The pain got to the point where I went in fear of the infections running throughout my body. The fear led me to think I needed to take an antibiotic. As I considered a very strong antibiotic, a third generation cephalosporin, my soul told me not to take it. But, I bought into the fear and took one of the blue pills. Within half an hour my whole body felt as if it was on fire and degeneration setting into my entire system.

As I felt this fire burning out my cells, I asked Spirit what was going on. The Spirit said that this antibiotic had degeneration codes energetically infused. These degeneration codes were put into these anti-biotics, to cause further degeneration of the body. The intent for putting in these degeneration codes, was to take severely infected human beings and allow them to pass to the other side. The third generation cephalosporin are generally restricted to people who have severe infections.

I didn't believe this was true. However, I felt like I had aged ten years in one night. The next day I called on a woman I knew who had a frequency device, similar to a rife machine, which could diagnose energetically what was going on in my body. She told me to come over and hooked me up to her machine. As I spoke into the computer it took the vibrations of my voice and told me exactly what was going on. To my amazement, it said cellular degeneration due to synthetic pharmaceutical. This was exactly what the spirit told me.

That night I again went into fear, and took another one of the blue pills. Again within half an hour, my entire body was again set on fire. Spirit whispered to me, "Take Sacred Journey," an amazon herbal homeopathic, which helps me to look at what's going on spiritually. I saw the degeneration codes and was told by Spirit to transmute (change them) the energy into regeneration codes. I was also told that the bacteria was only doing what it was coded within its genetics to do. It was coded to degenerate cellular material into its basic constituents of amino acids and minerals, so they can return to the earth and become food for the plants.

The spirit told me to recode the bacteria for regeneration of the tissue, so that they would help rebuild my thumb, instead of degenerating the thumb tissue.

As soon as my intent was set, and the thoughts and words were sent into motion, my thumb started to feel better. I thanked the bacteria for helping to rebuild my thumb.

I then looked at the antibiotic from a spiritual viewpoint, thanked it for being in my body and through my intent, changed its purpose to only help get rid of the infection and not cause degeneration of my cells. The burning and degeneration stopped. Healing began to set into my thumb and wrist.

Then, the Spirit told methat, in order to heal quickly, I needed to change my belief of going from point A to point B. to point C. to point D. to point E, in the healing process, that I should set my focal point, on point E of being totally healed, and not go through the entire process of healing. The Spirit said, "the focal point should be your only process".

In medical school, I was taught the three phases of healing. First is the inflammatory phase when the cells go through hemostasis and inflammation for a period of anywhere from 2 to 5 days. Then in the second phase or proliferative phase, the tissue will go through granulation, where fibroblasts lay a new layer of collagen which fills in the defects and produces new capillaries. Contraction of the tissue where the wound edges hold together takes place and reduces the defect. Epithelialization then crosses over the surface making new skin. The second phase can take up to two weeks. The third phase or remodeling phase, takes anywhere from three weeks to two years. New collagen and new tissue is placed and replaced during this phase and can cause scar tissue.

In order for my thumb to heal perfectly, without going through these three phases, and to heal perfectly without scar tissue, I needed to set my focus on the focal point of health, skipping all the various phases of wound healing.

Today I set my focal point for healing perfectly.

TODAY I BREATHE IN THE
ENERGY OF RE-GENERATION

B reathe in, with the intent to connect to the magma of the earth, Hold the breath for 10 seconds.
Breathe out, with the intent to let go of cellular degeneration codes.
Breathe in, to connect to the heavens, and bring in the cellular regeneration codes.
Breathe out, again with the intent to clear and let go of cellular degeneration codes.
Breathe in the prana (Sankrit word for "vital life"), and bring in the cellular regeneration codes.
Hold the breath for 10 seconds.
Breathe out, with the intent to clear the cellular membrane and let go of cellular degeneration codes.
Breathe in the prana, and bring in the cellular regeneration codes, thanking source energy for the regeneration and healing of the body.
Hold the breath for 10 seconds.
Breathe out, with the intent to clear and let go of cellular degeneration codes.
Breathe in again, bringing in the prana, and visualize the cells regenerating with the energy and filling the nucleus, DNA and RNA of the cells codes of regeneration.
Breathe out, releasing any energy slowing the healing process.
Breathe in again, focusing on light and love entering into all of the cells of the body, creating health, regeneration, hope, peace, bliss, love, and perfection.
Breathe out, releasing all doubts and fears.

Story time:

Trishia, a woman who worked at our Herb store, had broken the meta-tarsal of her foot dancing and jumping at a wedding for my sister-in-law, and was leaving to go to Peru. When her bone broke, severe pain set in, she started to panic, as her trip was only two days away. She asked, "What should I do?"

I expounded, "Do what I have taught you."

She sat down in the middle of some beautiful flowers with the intent to heal her foot, breathing in the prana, and sending regeneration to her foot.

Then, she did another technique I had taught her. Sending Love to the plants, earth, water, air, elementals surrounding her, she asked them to assist her healing. Trishia asked them to impart a small amount of their healing energy, not enough to injure them, but sufficient to heal the bone in her foot. She asked with faith, not doubting, and it was done.

Trishia then found me, smiling from ear to ear.

"My foot is healed", she stated.

My Medical training then surfaced. "We'd better get an exam by a doctor"

Trishia made an appointment for a massage instead, was seen by the massage therapist in a chiropractors office. The chiropractor, hearing her talk about her broken foot, asked her, "Would you like a free X-Ray ?"

After examining the X-Ray of her foot, he stated. "You diffinitly have a well healed old fracture in that area of your foot, four-six weeks into the healing process, but no new fracture is evident". "Did you break your foot a month or more ago?", he asked. Trishia smiled, "No, it was two days ago"!

Today I teach my body to respond to my questions, so I can receive answers for my health

Kinesiology, also known as human kinetics, is the scientific study of human movement. "Kinesi" is energy, "ology" is the study of. This scientific study includes many different modalities for using the human body to test eternal truths. Muscle testing, one of the first modalities, has been used for centuries with human beings. My first exposure with kinesiology, involved placing some sugar in a person's hand, and testing the person's strength, which was totally lost with the energy of the sugar in the field of the person being tested. It would work every time even with the most skeptical of people. I have also found, that telling the body to move forward for a yes answer, or move toward the object, if it is good for you, and away from the object, if it is bad for you, or backward for no. This application of kinesiology is a very good way to test foods, herbs, objects, and even people.

To do something like this, it is first necessary to set your intent, to decide what you desire your body to do. It won't just do it by itself, although movement does become automatic once you decide. So set your intention to move forward when it is a yes answer. Set your intention to move forward if it is something good for you. Set your intention to move away from the object if it is bad for you. Set your intention to move backward if it is no answer. I have always felt this is the easiest way to use kinesiology to test objects.

If you want to be more specific with something in front of you, you can point your finger at the object, or use your eyes to look directly at it. Our fingers project energy. That's why we we're taught when we we're young not to point at people. We were taught it was rude. We were taught the true energetics of pointing. When we point we are making a judgment, but we were never taught to follow through with that judgment.

Staring at people, with our eyes, was also taught to be rude. We are always sending out energy with our eyes and our fingers. Sometimes the energy we are sending out is judgmental and negative. We can use these energies to our advantage. You can focus on an object by pointing at it or looking at the object, and with your kinesiology, you can test whether the object is good or bad, a yes or a no. Your body will move forward for a yes, and if it is good for you, but move the body away, if it's a no or the object is bad for you.

With this ability you can easily confirm what you're hearing in your head. Always remember that your first thought is the intuitive answer. Any deeper thoughts bring in the ego, which can bring other answers that will not be from your soul. EGO meansEdging God Out.

Storytime:

When I first opened my herb shop, we brought in thousands of different herbs and other items. At that time, I didn't know the proper dosing or the properties of all the herbal and homeopathic products. Luckily I intuitively knew the core cause of disease within each person. I would take them into the herb and vitamin shop and I would ask one question,: "What is the optimal product to help get this person healthy?"

I had taught my body to move toward the products that would be best, but there were so many products, that I had to follow my body with the kinesiology. I would feel my body move toward the main shelf of the product category that they needed. Then I would test which shelf the product was on. I would point with my finger and I would feel my body move, when I was at the optimal product, then I would then take the product or herbs in my hand and ask, "What dosing would be the best for this person?" I would then in my mind think, "One … two… three… four… etc. When my body moved, I would know the right number of capsules, tablets or drops. Then I would use the same method to find the number of times per day the product should be taken. Again I would ask once, twice, thrice, etc. it would always test perfectly with the dosing and the amount of times per day to take the herbs.

Just like all healing modalities can be different for every person, there is a different way to use kinesiology to test and to get your answers. You just have to figure out which is the best way for testing for you.

TODAY I DE-TOX MY BODY

Detoxing is a lifelong process, and living in today's toxic environment requires us to be very vigilant in cleansing with the best products available.

Who needs to detox?

Every one!

How do we begin?

Intent is very important. Spiritually everything begins with our intention. Intention gives us a focal point. In other words, it gives us a goal, but more than that, it gives our energy direction and focus.

Ho-oponopono (**ho-o-pono-pono**) is an ancient Hawaiian practice of reconciliation and forgiveness. It starts the process of detoxing and cleaning our energy, clearing negative thoughts and emotions.

This is achieved by constant mindfulness and intent to clean negative thoughts and emotions. Cleaning is the actual Ho'oponopono practice. Cleaning what? You clean yourself from subconscious programs that run your life without your participation. The process of clearing and cleaning your energy, also helps those who affect you. It clears their energy also.

The Ho'oponopono process is very simple. It involves repetition of the following phrases:

- I Love You (focus unconditional Love towards yourself and others)
- Please forgive me (for whatever was done to bother you or them)
- I am sorry (for whatever was done to bother you or them)
- Thank you -- have gratitude for all your and their thoughts or actions and allow negative ones to disappear and un-create so the thought forms no longer affect either of you

With Ho'oponopono, cellular memory of negative emotions is released.

Cellular memory is the energetic imprint of emotions, whether positive or negative. Releasing cellular memory requires intent and purpose. Visualization of the release is very important.

Our bodies are like sponges. Every thought, every emotion, is absorbed into our cells. Then these energies incorporate into the membrane of the cell every organelle and into the mitichondria, clogging and choking the cells and the energetic flow. Good intent, good thoughts and the release of negative energies which will unclog the cells.

And detoxing can be fun. Imprinting new regenerating codes or thoughtforms into our cells and organs can be a pleasurable exercise.

Our body is very susceptible to thoughts, ideas and energetic imprints. We should be very careful what we accept as truth.

Accepting negative energies and negative thoughts affects our body. Through acceptance of these energies it incorporates into our cellular memory.

Cancel negative thoughts as soon as you recognize them. Stop them prior to them incorporating in the organ or cells of the body. This is done by saying "cancel" to negative statements or thoughts, saying out loud and making statements to the opposite of the negative thought. An example of this would be, "I am a afraid" then you would say "cancel that" or "I cancel fear, and replace it with faith, peace, joy, harmony." This is very effective and changes the energy before it incorporates into the cells.

Stop living unconsciously. Start living consciously and thinking positively.

Make constant positive choices with your intent and your actions.

If you desire to cleanse, stop taking toxins into your body. Start cleansing your body

If you desire to be healthy, make healthy choices.

Storytime:

I first encountered Ho'oponopono five years ago. I knew about many methods of healing.

Our son-in-Law was being sent to Afghanistan, our daughter was distraught with grief and sorrow. War, what is it good for? We were traveling home, feeling the heaviness. I wasn't paying attention to the speedometer, going ninety miles an hour.

Behind us, I see the lights blinking, telling me to slow down and pull over.

My wife, is horrified. Another problem in a day filled with sorrow.

I said, "Let's Ho'oponopono our thoughts right now."

We both started saying in our mind, "I Love you, I'm sorry, please forgive me, thank you for pulling me over" with the intent to go to the highway patrolman and clear the energy.

By the time he asked me to roll down the window, we were both sobbing.

He was a gentleman, about my same age. He looked at us sobbing and said, "What's wrong?"

Between the tears, we both started telling the story of traveling to Salt Lake City to send our son-in-law off to Afghanistan, I told him how I hadn't paid attention to the speed and I promised I would slow down.

The officer started to tell us about all the people in his life who had served the nation and of his patriotism. He told us uplifting stories from his own life and his children. He then, thanked us for the conversation and stated, "I'm glad I pulled you over, I was feeling nobody cared about our nation and it's people, and I am refreshed discussing your Love for our country and your son-in-law serving our nation. God Bless you, just drive safely."

He gave us a big grin and no ticket.

Today I Take Back My Health.

Stop living in the illusion that others have your health as their best interest.

Live each day as if everything you do, everything you eat, everything you breath, everything you drink, everything you say, and everything you accept as true, affects your health.

I've been practicing medicine for 28 years. My experiences have taught me, everyone needs to detox and no Medical Doctor will tell you to detox and clean up the environmental, emotional toxins in your body. They will usually prescribe another chemical to add to the toxic mess.

Physically detoxing takes commitment, but can be fun to do, too.

Set goals: With a practitioner of natural medicine, established a communication and a partnership. Preferably one who practices kinesiology. When I first started practicing chelation therapy, the dosing always tested with kinesiology, to start slow, at a lower dose. Even well trained alternative Medical doctors follow protochols, rather than reading into the body. Luckily, I always followed my intuition, using lower doses, and moving up when the body and kidneys were ready. Every patient is different. Every patient has needs of different dosing.

Cleaning up and reinvigorating the organs of elimination is of paramount importance. The colon, digestive system, liver, lymphatic's, skin, lungs and kidneys all help remove toxins from the body. Each of these organs should be supported and rebuilt while detoxing.

Inno-vita, Systemic Formulas, Standard Process, and many other professional herbal companies, have professionally blended herbal products which will assist, support, and rebuild, the organs of elimination. Kinesiology is the best way to test which organs need support. Blood testing only shows one moment in time, and I have found it to be highly in-accurate.

Many products on the market now, are excellent oral chelators. But they still need to be tested with kinesiology.

Meta-Ex.- This product from Inno-vita is an excellent oral chelator of heavy metals. It should be dosed mainly at bedtime as chelating out heavy metals may cause fatigue.

Tox-Ex- Another Product from a Inno-vita, is an excellent combination that helps remove unnatural petrochemicals, solvents, herbicides, pesticides, and insecticides, unnatural hormones and other chemicals from the body.

CLNZ this product is from Systemic Formulas and has properties of removing petrochemicals and heavy metals from the body.

The process of skin detoxing includes- foot baths with ionic electrolysis of water, mineral salt soaks, massage cleansing techniques, infrared sauna, bath soaks, skin masks and body masks. Far infrared and ultrasonic detox is also available.

Storytime :

When I was first undergoing my healing from cancer, I was told I needed to do chelation therapy. I had practicied and used this infusion therapy at Cardinal Glennon Hospital for children, in St. Louis Missouri.

We used a substance called EDTA to remove lead from children who were eating leaded paint and had lead poisoning. Most of these children also were diagnosed with a disease called Pica.

We would give them an IV with EDTA, a chemical first developed in Germany in the 1930's. This substance would chelate, or grasp onto, heavy metal molecules and bring the metals out of the body through the kidneys. It would also bring out some good molecules, which would be replaced at the end of the chelation sessions. Vitamins and minerals were added in the intravenous solution.

In Arizona at that time of my experience with the cancer, homeopathic and naturopathic physicians, osteopathic doctors were the only ones doing chelation therapy.

I sought out and started doing chelation therapy. The first few chelations, I was left with severe fatigue due to the strain on my kidneys. But, I found the more chelations I did, the more energy my body seemed to have.

Then I noticed I was remembering names of people- which had been a huge frustration for me as I could not remember the names of new acquaintances. This renewed memory capability, showed me that some marvelous things were happening within my nervous system, getting the lead and other heavy metals out. I also had "downwinder", radiation isotope poisoning from above ground nuclear bomb testing, other heavy metal, and chemical poisons. I started studying about these in my spare time. I found I could benefit from other natural substances such as chlorophyll, cilantro, N-Acetyl Cysteine, and many others.

My sister, Sharon, developed a metastatic hepato-sarcoma, two years after my malignant melanoma was cured. She choose to be treated the Medical route, with chemotherapy, surgery and radiation. Within eighteen months, she died from her treatment.

I have found detoxing, nutritional supplementation and chelation therapy with EDTA and natural substances to be very beneficial.

This can be done with the medical treatments suggested by your doctor and improve the outcome.

TODAY I BUILD MY FAITH

What is Faith? Biblically speaking, it's a belief in something I can't see, feel, hear, taste or touch. But if I have the faith the size of a mustard seed, I can move mountains.

Faith is belief that is not based on proof or double blinded studies

Faith is a focused belief, knowledge, power that builds from intent, and thought.

Faith builds as I add to the strength of my belief, intent and thought.

Faith changes belief into reality.

Faith transforms and transmutes energy.

The power of faith channels through to my soul and manifests into my emotional and mental bodies, and then into the physical self.

Faith builds with my thoughts and alignment with universal truth.

My Faith aligns me with the universe.

Faith healers, and natural healers, are born with or develop the power to assist me with channeling the healing energy from God or Source energy.

I am born with the ability, oportunity and task of increasing my Faith and power for helping heal myself, the tribe, the planet, the universe, all of humanity.

The Masters are called Masters, because they have Mastered the perfect channeling of Faith, transforming energy, thought and intent. They are in perfect alignment with the universe, omnipresent, omnipotent, with perfect knowledge.

Today, I increase my Faith, and heal, aligning myself with my highest good.

Story Time:

Three years ago, Vicki and our two youngest children vacationed on a cruise to Alaska, with a group from Hay House (Louis Hay's publishing company). One of my Favorite writers is Greg Braden, one of Vicki's is Carolyn Myss, We wanted to meet them on the trip. We said a little prayer, prior to departing with that intent, expressing Faith or believing it would happen.

Prior to departing, everyone on the ship, put on life vests and gather around their life boat. Vicki and the girls were put with the women, I was with the men. Greg Braden was on my left, Carolyn Myss was on Vicki's right side. We were both able to talk with our favorite authors for about forty minutes, right at the beginning of the cruise on the boat. Isn't Faith and manifestation wonderful? We certainly thought so!

The whole trip was filled with amazing healing and stories of Faith. As we were cruizing on the ship, we entered a fjord in Alaska where the Hubbard glacier was located. There was a thick fog and we were unable to even see the sides of the fjord. All of the people on the cruise were very spiritually oriented. It was our desire to clear the fog so we could see the glacier. A group of about 40 of us were up on the top deck manifesting to clear the fog. The power of the combined energies of those on the deck started to push the fog back away from the front of the boat and as we moved forward the fog was pushed back clear to the sides of the bay and it cleared in front of us totally. As we approached the glacier everyone cheered, we were all very happy and enjoyed the beauty and marvelous glacier and the mountains of Alaska in front of us.

When you express your faith, more miracles can manifest in the daily processes of your life!

TODAY I DO LONG DEEP BREATHING

Long Deep Breathing is an excellent way for one to become aware of the full distention and contraction of the diaphragm, after which kundalini breathing may come more naturally.

Sitting cross-legged (or even in corps pose, lying down), take in a long and deep breath. First fill the abdominal area by pushing the abdominal cavity out, using the diaphragm , to inhale the air down. Then pressing the air consciously into the lower abdomen. By arching somewhat forward with your palms on the knees, and then with arms straight pressing the palms inward towards the lower body against the knees, the chest cavity will open forwards, so that you can not only keep the pressure on the lungs but also in the lower abdominal area. You feel the lungs filling in filling with air and through the chest area. Finally, because of the forward arch of the spine, the upper area of the lungs will fill with air as well, all without the need to either open the rib cage or raise the shoulders.

Once the lungs are completely filled in this manner, hold the breath for ten seconds, pressing the shoulders back and expanding the chest out, so that the full length and pressure on the diaphragm can be felt.

Then slowly contract the entire length of the diaphragm from the upper chest to the abdomen, so that all the air is squeezed out.

By breathing in this way through the nostrils for several breaths, the flow of energy consciousness (prana, in Sanskrit) through the diaphragm can be felt from the pressing down and distending of the air into the lower region of the lungs, where most of the blood circulates, then filling through and up to the chest areas from the back to the front and into the upper lungs, filling those areas of the chest that are often not filled with air and prana.

The pressure in all areas of the lungs generates energy in all the nerve endings, so that the entire body is affected both by the breath and the pressure on the nerves.

When Long Deep Breathing is done in the manner described, the focus on expanding the muscles of the abdomen, chest and shoulder areas, opens up the circulation. The breathing brings in oxygen and prana, as the natural bellows like motion of the entire diaphragm is felt.

Storytime:

When I first started teaching breathing methods, the first was this deep breathing method, it was useful because it filled the lungs, diaphragm first (called diaphragmatic breathing). Then it fills the the upper areas of the chest as it is expanded. This is the original breathing of the ancients. In the early years of the earth before the industrialization and pollution, the oxygen content of the atmosphere was up above 40%. In some cities we are now down to 13 to 14% oxygen. There are also multiple other compounds and chemicals in the air we are breathing today. Having burned leaded gasoline for years, lead poisoning is prevalent all over the world. Our mothers all have lead poisoning, passed this lead through the placenta to us as babies.

Breathing with intent to clear toxins from the body is very important. Each breath we take we should have the intent of cleaning the air by moistening it in through the nose, then clearing our system by breathing out the toxins. But not only breathing out the toxins, but transmuting them into substances the earth can take and detox and put **back** into the ecosystem without pollution. As I would teach techniques of breathing, I would also teach the intent of the breathing and the purpose of the breathing.

When people are mindful, consciously breathing, we will help cleanse not only ourselves but our planet of the pollutants and become more aware of our environment.

TODAY I DO KUNDALINI BREATHING

The "root lock" is a conscious contraction of the pubo-coccygeus muscle or PC muscle which is a hammock-like muscle, found in both sexes, that stretches from the pubic bone to the coccyx (tail bone) It form the floor of the pelvic cavity and supports the pelvic organs. It is part of the levator ani group of muscles. When contracted it can stop the flow of urine and cut off our stool. Strengthening this muscle improves blood flow to the sexual organs and the root organs of the anus and the coccyx bone. The other important function of this muscle, it is very active during orgasm and sexual intercourse.

Tightening of this muscle and holding this pubo-coccygeus muscle tight is called the root lock. The sacrum and coccyx bones act as a fulcrum pump, circulating the cerebro-spinal fluid or central nervous system fluid. Each layer or each chakra going up the spine and into the head acts to circulate this cerebral-spinal fluid. Having the intent to make this fluid flow is very important with kundalini breathing.

I breathe in a deep breath and ground the root chakra into the earth preferably into the magma of the earth.

Then, I breathe out, and then another deep breath focusing energy on connecting to the heavens.

In craniosacral therapy, the coccyx and the sacrum act as a fulcrum, pumping cerebral spinal fluid of the anterior spinal column into the brain and around the posterior part of the brain down the posterior spinal column. Pushing or thrusting the pelvis forward, activates this pumping action.

Next take a big deep breath connected to the earth and the heavens and draw in the prana of the universe, locking the root lock as the breath comes in and pushing the pelvis and sacrum forward, holding the breath for ten seconds. As the breath is released the root lock is also released. This breath is then repeated at least two more times (can be done as many as I desire, but at least three times total for each chakra).

When I have completed at least three breaths with my root chakra doing the root lock each time as I breathe in and holding it till I release my breath, the energy is then brought up my body into the tongue, then the tongue placed at the roof of the mouth (mid-palate) bringing the energy up, I then roll my eyes up, lifting the energy with my hands high above my head bringing the energy with the hands and locking the energy into the ninth chakra eight to twelve inches above the head.

Next focus on the creative or sexual chakra. Take a big deep breath in through the nose again connected to the earth and the heavens and draw in the prana of the universe. This breath is focused on the sexual organs and a pelvic thrust is done as the breath is drawn in and held for ten seconds holding the root lock the entire time. As the breath is released the root lock is also released and the pelvis is brought back to a resting position. This is then repeated at least twice or more additional times taking care to lock the root lock and force the pelvis forward with each breath.

When I have completed at least three breaths with my pelvic chakra, doing the root lock each time as I breathe in and holding it till I release my breath, the energy is then brought up my body into the tongue, then the tongue placed to the roof of the mouth bringing the energy up and rolling the eyes up, taking the hands high above my head and locking the energy into the ninth chakra.

Focus next on the solar plexus or abdominal chakra. Take a big deep breath in through the nose connecting to the earth and the heavens and draw in the Love of the universe. This breath is focused on the abdominal organs of the liver, pancreas, spleen, intestines, stomach within this chakra. As the breath is brought in, turn the entire body, with the hands over the bellybutton, to the right and hold the root lock. The breath is held for ten seconds and then released as you turn to the left. The twisting motion should be right at the level of the solar plexus or just two finger breathes above the bellybutton. At least two additional breaths or more can be done at this level turning each time to the right and releasing when going to the left.

When I have completed at least three breaths with my solar plexis chakra doing the root lock each time as I breathe in and holding it till I release my breath, the energy is then brought up my body into the tongue, then the tongue placed at the roof of the mouth (mid-palate) bringing the energy up and rolling the eyes up, taking the hands high above my head bringing the energy with the hands and locking the energy into the ninth chakra, eight to twelve inches above my head.

The next level is the heart chakra. When breathing in, the body should be tilted to the right at the level of the heart and locking the root lock as the breath is coming again holding the breath for 10 seconds. The release the body should be tilted to the left root lock released as the breath is released. At least two additional breaths or more can be done at this level tilting to the right the breath coming in in the root lock locked leading for 10 seconds then tilting to the left and releasing.

When I have completed at least three breaths with my heart chakra, doing the root lock each time as I breathe in and holding it till I release my breath, the energy is then brought up my body into the tongue, then the tongue placed at the roof of the mouth (mid-palate) bringing the energy up and rolling the eyes up, taking the hands high above my head bringing the energy with the hands and locking the energy into the ninth chakra, eight to twelve inches above my head.

The next level is the level of the throat chakra. With this breath when breathing into the body from the universe and the earth, the shoulders are lifted when breathing in and the root lock tightened. This is held for 10 seconds and then released as we were lower the shoulders and release the root lock. This is repeated two more times lifting the shoulders up and tightening the root lock with the breath in for 10 seconds and then releasing the root lock in the shoulders at the end of the breath.

When I have completed at least three breaths with my throat chakra, doing the root lock each time as I breathe in and holding it till I release my breath, the energy is then brought up my body into the tongue, then the tongue placed at the roof of the mouth (mid-palate) bringing the energy up and rolling the eyes up, taking the hands high above my head bringing the energy with the hands and locking the energy into the ninth chakra, eight to twelve inches above my head.

The next level is at the level of the third eye or pituitary chakra. This chakra will be rotated starting to the rights bringing in the breath, locking the root lock and slowly rotating the head to the back and then releasing as it goes to the left and comes forward releasing the breath and the root lock. This is repeated two more times or more if desired, rotating the head to the right as the breathing comes in and locking the root lock and then releasing the root lock and the breath as the rotation goes forward on the left side. This should be done in a rotating fashion as to rotate the cerebral spinal fluid.

When I have completed at least three breaths with my third eye chakra, doing the root lock each time as I breathe in and holding it till I release my breath, the energy is then brought up my body into the tongue, then the tongue placed at the roof of the mouth (mid-palate) bringing the energy up and rolling the eyes up, taking the hands high above my head bringing the energy with the hands and locking the energy into the ninth chakra, eight to twelve inches above my head.

The next level is the level of the celestial chakra or pineal gland chakra. Intent should be to bring in the prana of heaven and the earth with the prana and breath as the head is tilted back and arms extended back as if spreading out a set of wings with your arms and your head is held back.

The breath is held for ten seconds with the energy entering into your pineal gland and then released as the arms are brought forward and the head is tilted forward. If your neck is stiff or if this is painful, be gentle to yourself and your neck. It is important that comfort and bliss accompany this breathing. This breath should be repeated two or more times bringing the arms and head back gently bringing in the prana and the breath and holding the root lock locked and releasing the root lock and releasing the breathe bringing the arms forward and the head forward.

When I have completed at least three breaths with my cerebral chakra, doing the root lock each time as I breathe in and holding it till I release my breath, the energy is then brought up my body into the tongue, then the tongue placed at the roof of the mouth (mid-palate) bringing the energy up and rolling the eyes up, taking the hands high above my head bringing the energy with the hands and locking the energy into the ninth chakra, eight to twelve inches above my head.

This is a gentle exercise. If any of the root locks or chakra's cause pain, the actions should be minimized and gently done till discomfort or pain is gone.

The energy stored in my ninth chakra is there or for my use to heal my body or to heal someone else should I choose. This energy is released with my intent to release the energy and brought down into any part of the body to heal. I can give myself energy, as needed, or heal an organ that is particularly causing problems. I can also throw the energy to someone else using my hands if they are in need.

Storytime:

Our daughter was living in Tooele, Utah and had decided to move back home. My wife went up to help her move, and was driving home to southern Utah when she experienced severe fatigue and felt like the flu was coming on with severe headache and body aches. She called me to talk to her as she continued driving home to keep her awake and safe. I had just talked about the kundalini breathing and had stored the energy in my ninth chakra. The thought came to me to just send her that energy, to help her stay awake and drive home safely. I took my hands and put them above my head releasing a ball of energy and I threw to her in Beaver, Utah. She was still on the phone and I asked her how she felt. She said all of a sudden her energy had improved and she was no longer sleepy. I told her to call me again if she needed the energy. She safely drove home with plenty of energy over the next two hours. What ever is going on in your life or the life of your loved ones, this energy is readily available for you. It also can be used for what ever your body is lacking or desires.

I also have a CD explaining and doing the kundalini breathing and audio. This is available for those who need an audio explanation of the kundalini breathing.

TODAY I FIND A 'HANDS ON' HEALER

Today, to help me heal, I am to go to a hands-on healer, who will open up blocked energy flow, get my bio-meridians working, and channel the perfect energy from the universe into my body balancing my Chi or energy.

Hands-on healing, also known as Healing Energy, Radiant or Spiritual Healing, has been practiced by many cultures for thousands of years

There are several kinds of hands-on healers:

Reiki is a Japanese technique for stress reduction and relaxation that also promotes

healing. It's administered by laying on of hands, or placing the hands closely to the body transferring energy from the universe through thought, colors, vibrations, sacred geometry and symbols. It can be easily learned by anyone.

There are first, second and third degree Reiki Masters, who have trained and learned about sacred geometry and moving energy through symbols and ancient rhythms and frequencies.

Massage Therapists are also trained in the art of hands-on healing. I ask them to include energy work for assisting the body to heal and for energy or chi balancing.

Hands of Light Practitioners, after the Barbara Brennan style.

This practitioner has studied methods of rebalancing the chakras using touch, movement, and techniques which involve removing negative energy out of the body and restoring or replacing positive energy into the spiritual, mental, emotional and physical bodies.

Story Time:

When I first met my wife Vicki, we were having various healers instruct their methods of healing at my office. I had studied Reiki and completed the 3rd degree, or Reiki Master, Vicki had studied the Barbara Brennan method. We both had studied Reflexology and other techniques for healing. With all the stress of going through divorce, changes in occupation, and children being sick, we found ourselves doing healing sessions each night. For any family member whom felt ill or we felt needed hands on healing energy, we would place a blanket on the floor, have them lay down and we would start removing negative energy, with one person at the head of the body, one person in the middle and another at the feet, pulling bad energy out, giving it to the earth to transmute the energy back into good energy. This kept the family healthy during a very difficult time. I know our children, they will never forget those special times together, doing healing.

Today I Start a Two Week Parasite Cleanse

Today I will start a two-week parasite cleanse with black walnut, wormwood and cloves. I will also add plant enzymes to break up the mucus and cellular membrane the body puts around to wall off the parasites. I'll use Tetra cleanse or other supplement which supports the liver, kidneys, and digestive system. Tetra cleanse will also clean up the dead bodies and help dispose the toxins released by the parasites.

Each day, for the entire two weeks, I will take plant enzymes six in the morning and six at bedtime. I like the NOW plant enzymes because there is a sufficient amount of cellulase to break down cell walls. I will take four tetra cleanse at bedtime each night during the parasite cleanse and the last dose, the night after completion of the two weeks. (15 nights total)

Hulda Clark taught that a parasite cleanse should start slowly at lower doses the first few days, to keep from having such a large 'die off' of parasites. (Fast die-off can cause reactions including herxheimer reaction)

Day one: just one drop of the black walnut extract four times a day, morning lunch, dinner, and bedtime. One capsule of cloves, three times a day, Morning, dinner and bedtime. One capsule wormwood, just prior to dinner. 6 capsules Plant Enzymes first thing in the morning, 6 capsules at bedtime. Tetra cleanse 4 capsules at bedtime.

Day two take two drops of the black walnut extract morning, lunch, dinner, and bedtime but cloves should be taken two morning, dinner and bedtime and two wormwood prior to dinner. Plant Enzymes 6 capsules first thing in the morning and , 6 capsules at bedtime. Tetra cleanse 4 capsules at bedtime.

<u>Day three:</u> take three drops of black walnut extract under the tongue morning, lunch, dinner, and bedtime. Cloves, three capsules morning, dinner, and bedtime. Three capsules wormwood prior to dinner. Plant Enzymes 6 capsules first thing in the morning and , 6 capsules at bedtime. Tetra cleanse 4 capsules at bedtime.

<u>Day four</u> four drops of black walnut extract under the tongue, morning lunch, dinner, and bedtime. Cloves: three in the morning, at dinner, and at bedtime. Four wormwood prior to dinner. Plant Enzymes: six capsules first thing in the morning and six capsules at bedtime. Tetra cleanse, four capsules at bedtime.

<u>Day five:</u> five drops of black walnut extract under the tongue, morning lunch, dinner, and bedtime. Cloves: three in the morning, at dinner, and at bedtime. Five wormwood prior to dinner. Plant Enzymes: six capsules first thing in the morning and six capsules at bedtime. Tetra cleanse, four capsules at bedtime

<u>Day six</u> six drops of black walnut extract under the tongue, morning lunch, dinner, and bedtime. Cloves: three in the morning, at dinner, and at bedtime. Six wormwood prior to dinner. Plant Enzymes: six capsules first thing in the morning and six capsules at bedtime. Tetra cleanse, four capsules at bedtime.

<u>Day seven:</u> seven drops of black walnut extract under the tongue, morning lunch, dinner, and bedtime. Cloves: three in the morning, at dinner, and at bedtime. Seven wormwood prior to dinner. Plant Enzymes: six capsules first thing in the morning and six capsules at bedtime. Tetra cleanse, four capsules at bedtime.

<u>Day eight:</u> eight drops of black walnut extract under the tongue, morning lunch, dinner, and bedtime. Cloves: three in the morning, at dinner, and at bedtime. Eight wormwood prior to dinner. Plant Enzymes: six capsules first thing in the morning and six capsules at bedtime. Tetra cleanse, four capsules at bedtime.

<u>Day nine</u> : nine drops of black walnut extract under the tongue, morning lunch, dinner, and bedtime. Cloves: three in the morning, at dinner, and at bedtime. Nine wormwood prior to dinner. Plant Enzymes: six capsules first thing in the morning and six capsules at bedtime. Tetra cleanse, four capsules at bedtime.

Day ten: ten drops of black walnut extract under the tongue, morning lunch, dinner, and bedtime. Cloves: three in the morning, at dinner, and at bedtime. Ten wormwood prior to dinner. Plant Enzymes: six capsules first thing in the morning and six capsules at bedtime. Tetra cleanse, four capsules at bedtime.

Day eleven: eleven drops of black walnut extract under the tongue, morning lunch, dinner, and bedtime. Cloves: three in the morning, at dinner, and at bedtime. Elenven wormwood prior to dinner. Plant Enzymes: six capsules first thing in the morning and six capsules at bedtime. Tetra cleanse, four capsules at bedtime.

Day twelve: twelve drops of black walnut extract under the tongue, morning lunch, dinner, and bedtime. Cloves: three in the morning, at dinner, and at bedtime. Four wormwood prior to dinner. Plant Enzymes: six capsules first thing in the morning and six capsules at bedtime. Tetra cleanse, four capsules at bedtime.

Day thirteen: thirteen drops of black walnut extract under the tongue, morning lunch, dinner, and bedtime. Cloves: three in the morning, at dinner, and at bedtime. Thirteen wormwood prior to dinner. Plant Enzymes: six capsules first thing in the morning and six capsules at bedtime. Tetra cleanse, four capsules at bedtime.

Day fourteen: fourteen drops of black walnut extract under the tongue, morning lunch, dinner, and bedtime. Cloves: three in the morning, at dinner, and at bedtime. Fourteen wormwood prior to dinner. Plant Enzymes: six capsules first thing in the morning and six capsules at bedtime. Tetra cleanse, four capsules at bedtime.

Day fifteen: take two plant enzyme capsules prior to each meal and the four tetra cleanse capsules at bedtime.

Story time :

Twenty six years ago I was diagnosed with invasive malignant melanoma. My doctor friends informed me that chemotherapy and radiation were not an option, as Melanoma was resistant to such treatments; surgery would surely paralyze or damage my brain or spinal column. This left me no options, and my colleagues gave me approximately three months to get my house in order prior to an untimely death. In my heart, I felt I wasn't going to die, that I would find a way to cure this 'cancer'.

That night, I said a prayer, with faith in God, that I would find a cure for 'my' cancer (notice the 'my;' I was taking on the cancer as mine). That night, I had a dream, about a woman by the name of Hulda Clark, who gave me instructions on how to cure my cancer.

I went to work that morning knowing that I was going to beat this illness. To my astonishment an article was on my desk, by Dr. Hulda Clark, out of Chicago, Illinois, a PhD microbiologist stating in the article, that parasites are the cause of cancer. Her name and telephone number were at the end of the article,

I called the number and Dr. Hulda Clark answered the phone. I spoke with her about my condition for about ninety minutes, including my life-style and nutrition (or lack thereof). She will told me to stop drinking my six pack of soda pop a day, eat a "live food" diet, start her two week parasite cleanse, and do the two week parasite cleanse every three months for the rest of my life. I was to take esiac tea with cat's claw and start chelation therapy to remove heavy metal and toxins. She said 'sugar' was feeding the cancer, and to treat sugar like a poison for my body. I immediately started doing everything as we had discussed and within three months instead of being dead, I felt better than I had felt the last four years.

I lost 40 pounds in the process, and being an OB/GYN physician, all the women in my practice started asking what I had done to lose so much weight. I told them about the Parasite Cleanse and they all wanted to start the process to lose weight. I started them on the parasite cleansing, esiac Tea with cat's claw, etc., each and every one not only lost weight, but their polycystic ovaries, breast cysts, endometriosis, dysmenorrhea (painful periods), menorrhagia (heavy periods), dysparunia, (painful sex) improved and even became a nonissue. I was amazed that I hadn't learned about this in medical school and wondered why other physicians didn't know.

When I started discussing this with other physicians, the answers came. Modern medicine is run by corporations whose intent is to make money not heal the sick. The physicians told me not to mess around with herbs as it would eventually get me in trouble. Their prediction was correct.

Instead of another story---this is the Parasite cleanse

Take all herbs on an empty stomach <u>20 minutes prior to meals.</u>

Some Parasites require special Herbal Blends not listed below. Always seek help from a Herbal Professional familiar with your particular health concerns

Frankincense Oil or WO Chinese Healing oil: touched to the tongue four times a day with each dose of herbs

Take all Herbs till gone and preferably 20 minutes prior to eating. I feel it would be good for you to do

Oral Chelation, which is good to do with Parasite Cleasing, as Parasites take on some of the Toxic load and release it when they die.

Oral Chelation will remove heavy Metals and toxins from your body which are slowing your healing process.

Plant Enzymes (NOW herbs) 6 capsules first thing <u>in the morning</u> and <u>6 at night.</u> Breaks up mucous and cellular membranes, which form around parasites to wall them off.

Tetra Cleanse (Solaray) 4 casules at bedtime. Drink at least <u>8 full</u> cups of water a day.

Health & Longevity, Inc.
157 East Riverside Drive, St. George, UT 84790
(435) 986-0025
Scott R. Werner, M.D.

Instructions for parasite cleanse

Week 1	Day 1	Day 2	Day 3	Day 4	Day 5	Day 6	Day 7
Date	☐	☐	☐	☐	☐	☐	☐
Black Walnut Extract	1 drop x 4	2 drops x 4	3 drops x 4	4 drops x 4	5 drops x 4	6 drops x 4	7 drops x 4
Cloves	1 capsule x 1	2 caps x 2	3 caps x 3	3 caps x 3	3 caps x 3	3 caps x 3	3 caps x 3
Wormwood	1 before dinner	2 before dinner	3 before dinner	4 before dinner	5 before dinner	6 before dinner	7 before dinner

Week 2	Day 8	Day 9	Day 10	Day 11	Day 12	Day 13	Day 14
Date	☐	☐	☐	☐	☐	☐	☐
Black Walnut Extract	8 drops x 4	9 drops x 4	10 drops x 4	11 drops x 4	12 drops x 4	13 drops x 4	14 drops x 4
Cloves	3 caps x 3	3 caps x 3	3 caps x 3	3 caps x 3	3 caps x 3	3 caps x 3	3 caps x 3
Wormwood	8 before dinner	9 before dinner	10 before dinner	11 before dinner	12 before dinner	13 before dinner	14 before dinner

Take **Plant Enzymes** 6 first thing <u>in the morning</u> and <u>6 at night</u>
Tetra Cleanse 4 at bedtime
Drink at least <u>8 full</u> cups of water a day
Take all <u>Herbs</u> on an empty stomach <u>20 minutes prior to meals.</u>

TODAY I DO THE 'MASTER CLEANSE' FOR 24 HOURS

Iwill start by squeezing two fresh lemons into a gallon of fresh blessed filtered or tap water, add 2 tablespoons of grade B. maple syrup, 1/4 teaspoon of cayenne pepper, 1 tsp of Himalayan or Real sea salt. Drink the entire gallon today. Drink it whenever you are hungry instead of food

The master cleanse will do several things for you. You will drink a gallon of water, blessed water.

Lemons are a weak acid, which converts through the enzymatic processes of the body into a strong neutralizer. This makes my body's pH become more alkaline. This switches me into a more healing environment for the body and helps the blood and liver detox. Cayenne pepper helps the circulation, has Vitamin C and biophlavenoids. The pink Himalayan or Real sea salt puts electrolyts back into my body and has more potassium and trace metals than table salt. Do not use iodized salt.

Grade B. maple syrup, has B-vitamins, good complex sugars, which will clear and help detox the liver A Peppermint tea bag or two may be added to help with taste. Some people need a laxative tea if constipated. The book on the Master Cleanse is also an excellent reference.

All of the above pitured products are excellent for the master cleanse, some are carried in the Health & Longevity, Inc. herbal store or your favorite Herb Store. Please call if you have questions or need product sent to you at 435-986-0025.

MASTER CLEANSE INGREDIENTS 19.09.2012

Storytime:

About twelve years ago, when I was still using IV EDTA chelation treatments, an emaciated woman with a swollen belly, who had done twenty chelations due to heavy metal toxicity, was having trouble with her bowels and absorption of nutrients. I suggested the Master cleanse. She would do it on odd numbered days, and would eat organic vegetables and proteins with enzymes on the even days. Within two weeks, her belly normalized.

TODAY I START A 30 DAY YEAST/ FUNGAL CLEANSE WITH HERBS TO REBUILD MY GLANDS

Yeast/fungus has become a major problem in our society as a result of our eating too many processed sugars. Spores and molds travel in the air, food and water entering in the body. Yeast/fungus are aspirated into the lungs causing chronic coughs, asthma, difficulty breathing, and sleep apnea. In the digestive tract the fungus/yeast creates esophageal reflux, dyspepsia, bloating, heart burn, gas, poor absorption of nutrients, loss of good flora (bacteria), causes constipation, mucus and flatus to debilitate us. The yeast/fungus invade the glands and organs causing then to slow them down by sucking out the energy like little vampires. I believe fungus causes the organs to age and degenerate prematurely. When Fungus/yeast gets into the brain, it causes poor memory, brain fog, and later chronic illnesses such Alzheimer's, Parkinson's, and Lou Gehrig's disease, multiple sclerosis and other myelin sheath diseases.

Since yeast/fungus is very adaptable, anti-fungal cleanses should be changed prior to 42 days after which the yeast/fungus adapts and the antifungals become less effective. The best antifungal I've ever found, the #4 product called FungDX from Systemic Formulas kills and removes Fungus from the body. Adding Tai Ra Chi (another Systemic Formulas product) prevents mutagenic fungus. This combination of energized products is the one I use the most because I found it to be effective for even black fungus. In this book, you will find several references for you to take a Yeast/fungus cleanse. If you are currently within the 30 days of a fungal cleansing, opening the book to these pages states that you probably ought to continue for an additional 30 days, but possibly shift to a yeast/fungal cleanse with a different formulation.

Systemic formulas #4 Fung DX one capsule morning, lunch, dinner, and bedtime. We will also add Tai Ra Chi (translated 'Energy from God') and work on the glands as these are involved with fungus.

Inno-Vita Professional Herbal Products, Kreoger Herbs, Standard Process or other herbal professional products can be substituted. I use the products which test with intuition or Kinesiology the best for you. Use your personal health advisor if needed, with food and a good probiotic. (The following is just an example)

Product	Morning	Lunch	Dinner	Bed	Qty.	Cost
Ga Adrenal	2 caps				1	($22.00
Gf Thyroid		2 capsules			1	($22.00
Gt Thymus			2 capsules		1	($26.00
Gb Pituitary			2 capsules		1	$25.00
Tai Ra Chi	½ dropper	½ dropper	½ dropper		1	$24.00
#4 FungDx	1 capsule	1 capsule	1 capsule	1 capsule	2	($52for both
With food take i-Flora (Sedona)	The 1 capsule	Following	Probiotic or your 1 capsule	Own	1	($34.99

This will last 30 days. It will get the fungus reduced in the system. It's a good start.

It took four years to get the fungus/yeast under control in my system. Sugar feeds and strengthens fungus in the body. Avoid sugars, white breads, pastas and white vegetables as these become sugars in the body.

Storytime:

One of the first women who I started on a antifungal with glandular's regime was 53 years old, had gone through menopause, and wanted another child. She had had 12 children, and the 13th had come to her in a dream desiring to come into the family. She heard that I was very good with helping people unable to get pregnant, to get pregnant.

I told her that she would need to do eight chelation therapies, and do anti-fungal herbs for six months and at the same time strengthen her glands which were filled with fungus. She did two chelation therapies a month, and started taking the antifungal's with the glandular's. In the fifth month she became pregnant. We finished up the last two months of the antifungals and glandular's, because the herbals are very safe, the yeast/fungus would've caused the child health problems.

TODAY I START A 90 DAY YEAST/FUNGAL CLEANSE AND HERBS TO RESTORE/ REBUILD MY LIVER AND PANCREAS

Fungus can cause tremendous problems in the liver and pancreas, increasing cholesterol and diabetes risk. For this reason today you should start on an anti-yeast/fungal cleanse. You should also take herbs to cleanse and rebuild your liver and pancreas.

The liver has three main functions for the body. The first function is to produce the blood and produce enzymes and proteins for building and repairing cells within the body and making the blood. The second function is cleaning and detoxing the blood, and lymph. The third function is to make bile and store it in the gallbladder to be used when eating meals to breakdown and absorb fats from the intestines in the digestive process.

The pancreas, on the other hand, produces enzymes to help digest proteins, starches, fats and carbohydrates in the digestive process and produces insulin for the absorption and transport of glucose into the cells. When these organs have fungus in them, diabetes can ensue. The liver gets congested and fatty, start making more cholesterol, the bile thickens (sludge) and slows down the inner somatic processes of the liver. With thickened bile, the gallbladder spasms causing pain and subsequent removal. (Gallstones are caused by Parasitic infestations of the liver)

The following cleanse will help remove fungus from the liver, gallbladder, and pancreas, restoring function to the organs. Several companies have great products, but these two are what I test with intuition as especially good.

Systemic formulas #4 formula FungDX one capsule morning lunch dinner and bedtime LS liver stabilizer two capsules each morning, Lb liver gallbladder formula two capsules at lunch, Ps pancreatic stabilizer, two capsules at dinner and L liver two capsules at bedtime. There are 60 capsules in each bottle so you will need two #4 FungDx and ask for one bottle of each of the other formulas. If you turn to this page again, it means you should continue antifungal products. But help the Liver and Pancreas. . Inno-Vita Herbs, Standard process or other herbal professional products can be substituted. I use the products which test with intuition or Kinesiology the best for you. Use your personal health advisor if needed.

with food and a good probiotic. (The following is just an example)

1 st 30 days from Systemic Formulas

With food: 1 scoop Accell therapeutic in 16 ounces juice or water each morning 1 $70.00

Start with empty stomach	Morning	Lunch	Dinner	Bedtime	QTY	Cost
Ls Liver stabilizer	2 caps				1	($22.00
Lb Liver/ Gallblad		2 capsules			1	18.00
Ps Pancreas			2 capsules		1	($22.00
L Liver				2 capsules	1	$16.00
#4 FungDx	1 capsule	1 capsule	1 capsule	1 capsule	2	($52for both
With food take	The	Following				
ABC fornula or other probiotic	1 capsule		1 capsule		1	

2 nd 30 days from Inno-Vita

With food: 1 scoop Lepterra in 16 ounces juice or water each morning 1 $70

Start with empty stomach	Morning	Lunch	Dinner	Bedtime	QTY	Cost
Livergy	2 caps				1	
Gall-Astic		2 capsules			1	
Pancreos			2 capsules		1	
Tox-Ex				2 capsules	1	
Phung-Ex	1 capsule	1 capsule	1 capsule	1 capsule	2	
MetaEx				2 capsules	1	
With food take or other probiotic	The 1 capsule	Following 1 capsule				

3 rd 30 days from Systemic Formulas

With food: 1 scoop Accell therapeutic in 16 ounces juice or water each morning 1 $70.00

Start with empty stomach	Morning	Lunch	Dinner	Bedtime	QTY	Cost
Ls Liver stabilizer	2 caps				1	($22.00
Lb Liver/ Gallblad		2 capsules			1	18.00
Ps Pancreas			2 capsules		1	($22.00
L Liver				2 capsules	1	$16.00
#4 FungDx	1 capsule	1 capsule	1 capsule	1 capsule	2	($52for both
With food take i-Flora (Sedona) or other probiotic	The 1 capsule	Following 1 capsule		1		($34.99

Today I start a 90 day total body detox/cleanse with herbs to remove toxins and rebuild my organs of elimination, my liver, lymph, digestive system, cell membranes and cellular organelles, especially mitocondria

Hormone imbalances, heavyness of the eyes, chronic sinusitis, anxious feelings, fuzzy brain, headaches, digestive disorders, celiac disease and IBS (Gluten Enteropathy and Irritable Bowel syndrome or sensitivity), fatigue, trouble sleeping, Cancers, chronic inflammatory conditions, "Auto-immune dis-ease" are all due to negative emotions, petrochemicals, heavy metals, parasites,pathologic bacteria, virus and fungus in your system. Cellular and mitochondrial membrane toxicity is chronic fatigue. We repair and turn on, the organs of elimination first (Liver, Digestive tract, Colon and Kidneys) and restore function to the lymph and cellular matrix,which are the first two months (phases), then remove the biochemical toxins from the cell membranes and mitochondrial membranes with the ROX, EPIC, DV3, MORS, Vista and ENRGY which were made to unbind these pseudo-hormones, toxic proteins and chemical toxins from the cells and mitochondrial membranes, so they can function at optimal levels. These products are from Systemic Formulas. The Detoxification process Can be done in 60 days, however, to avoid Herxheimer reaction (Cleansing too quickly), I recommend 90 days.

90 day three phase detoxing of organs of elimination and cells. **Detoxification Program.**

1st Phase 30 days Do the following first (Day 1-30) Prepare organs of Elimination

With food: 1/4 scoop Accell therapeutic in 16 ounces juice or water each morning 1 $70.00

Start with empty stomach	Morning	Lunch	Dinner	Bedtime	QTY	Cost
Ls Liver stabil	2 caps				1	$22
D Digest	1 caps		1 capsule		1	$28
C Colon	1 caps		1 capsule		1	$19
ACX Vit-Detox	1 caps		1 capsule		1	$28
CLNZ (chelator)				1 capsule	1	$24.00
MoRS MethyDoner		1 capsule			1	$40.00
eNRG (ATP)		1 capsule			1	$40.00
Lb Liver/Gall			2 capsules		1	$18
L Liver Builder				2 capsules	1	$16

2nd Phase 30 days Next continue with this: (days 31-60) Cleanse the Extra-Cellular Matrix

With food: 1/4 scoop Accell therapeutic in 16 ounces juice or water each morning (already has)

Start with empty stomach	Morning	Lunch	Dinner	Bedtime	QTY	Cost
Ls Liver stabilizer	1 capsule				1	$22
D Digest	1 capsule		1 capsule		1	$28
C Colon	1 capsule		1 capsule		1	$19

ACX Vit-Detox	1 capsule		1 capsule		1	$28
CLNZ (chelator)				1 capsule	1	(already has)
REL (Chlorella)	1 capsule				1	$25
eNGY		1 capsule			1	$40
#1 Activator			One		1	$20.00
Gb Pituitary			2 capsules		1	$25.00
Lb Liver/Gall			1 capsule		1	$18
L Liver Build				1 capsule	1	$16
Ks Kidney s				1 capsule	1	$18

3rd Phase 30 days (days 61-90) Cleanse the Cellular Membrane and internal Cellular organelles

With food: 1/4 scoop Accell therapeutic in 16 ounces juice or water each morning

Start with empty stomach	Morning	Lunch	Dinner	Bedtime	QTY	Cost
Ls Liver s	1 capsule					Already has
Lb Liver Lb		1 capsule				Already has
L Liver			1 capsule			Already has
REL (Chlorella)	1 capsule				1	Already has
DV3	2 capsules				1	$26.00
Ks Kidney			1 capsule			Already has
eNGY		1 capsule			1	Already has

Epic Meta no/ono	1 capsule		1 capsule		1	$40.00
MORS Methylato	1 capsule		1 capsule		1	$40.00
ROX anti-oxidati	1 capsule		1 capsule		1	$40.00
Vista Liguid	1/2 dropper			1/2 dropper	1	$26.00
Vista Membrane regeneration	1 softgel		1 capsule		1	$30.00

I have also used the products from Inno-vita which do well with vegans. There is a special protochol for these products. Call 435 986-0025 to have these regimes e-mailed to you.

TODAY I BREATHE IN THE LOVING, COMPASSIONATE, PEACEFUL, REGENERATING ENERGY OF SOURCE.

I start my day by connecting to the earth with my breath, putting my energy deep into the magma. I then breathe up into the source energy, which is brightest most beautiful light in the universe. I imagine taking a piece of that energy, and bring it down into the center of my chest and my heart.

I exhale through my mouth. Then I take a deep breath through my nose. I focus in that small piece of source energy, expand it in my chest to the size of my heart, completely encompassing my heart light and love and peace. Then I breathe out.

Next I take a deep breath through the nose and began to expand the source energy and light to encompass my entire chest cavity, which is filled with light and love, bliss and harmony. Then I breathe out.

Next I take a deep breath through my nose, feeling my chest fill with beautiful light and love and expanding the source energy, out to the outermost part of my aura, filling up my entire body and the area surrounding me with love and hope , bliss and peace, abundance and health. I then breathe out through my mouth.

Next I taken a deep breath in through my nose, and feel the entire's city I'm living in, filling the city with love and light, prosperity, abundance and peace. Everyone in the city is experiencing the same feelings and sensations that I am experiencing. The city is full of love and light and peace. Then I breathe out through my mouth.

Then I take a deep breath through my nose, and feel the source energy, the light and love expanding into my entire country where I'm living. My whole country is peaceful, filled with love and light, prosperity, abundance. Everyone has the food they need and the water that they desire to drink which is purified and refreshing. Then I breathe out through my mouth.

Then I take a deep breath through my nose and feel that source energy fill the entire planet Earth with love and light, prosperity and abundance. The planet has flow of energy throughout, the plants, animals, insects are filled with love and light, have shelter, food and water to their contentment. The planet is vibrating with unconditional love and compassion. Then I breathe out through my mouth.

And then I taken a deep breath through my nose deal that source energy filling up the entire solar system, the sun and the planets and all the asteroids fill with compassion, unconditional love and light. Everything is rotating in perfection and all the planets are filled with the flow of perfect energy. Then I breathe out through my mouth.

Then I take a deep breath through my nose and feel the energy expanding out into the entire Milky Way galaxy and then into the entire universe.. It is filled with love and light, compassion and unconditional love. Everything is perfect. The entire universe is at peace. Then I breathe out through my mouth.

Storytime:

I was teaching about breathing. This breathing technique came to me from a past life when I was a sitta, and was teaching other monks about breathing techniques. It was amazing how it flowed to me and I revealed this technique to the people who were there to be taught about breathing. Each one of us could feel the expansion of the energy in our chests, and then in our city, and then in our state and our country, our world, and then finally in our universe. The entire group experienced love and peace and went home and slept in harmony with the universe. Every time I have done this breathing and taught it to others the experience has been the same. We should do this breathing technique at least once a week.

TODAY I RESET MY BODY TO HEAL

Resetting the body is not a new concept. The Pharaohs of ancient Egypt would go into the Kings' chamber of the great pyramid in Gaza, lie a sarcophagus built specifically to focus the energy of the pyramid to help repair and reset their tissue. This energy of the pyramid was so powerful that it would bring in energy to cleanse the cells and rejuvenate organs. According to one author, the energy would lengthen the telomeres, repairing DNA, RNA and mitochondrial function, essentially stopping the aging process. The cellular membrane would also be regenerated and toxins cleansed. The Pharaoh, as long as he was in tune, would open the body to these healing wavelengths, energies and vibrations, his body renewed and reinvigorated with energy from the heavens.

Today we live in a world where EMFs electromagnetic frequencies are disrupting our DNA and RNA, Retro-viruses designed to enter and cause dis-ease, enter into our cells or into the organs, our bodies are barely able to keep up with the damage, let alone repair and restore function.

Our food must be blessed, our water must be blessed, our bodies must be blessed.

But how can we go about blessing and rejuvenating our bodies?

One way is to undergo ancient rituals, meditations and prayer. Rituals at specific ages, bar mitzvah, christening, baptism, confirmation, laying on of hands to heal, or going to shaman, massage therapists, and practitioners of the healing arts. Adjusting our energy and giving thoughts of wholeness to our bodies, giving us the frequencies and energy we need to heal. I'm an advocate for taking the herbs, plants, teas, essential oils, homeopathic remedies which receive the energy of the air, of the sun (Fire), water and earth that rejuvenate and restore our cellular matrix. From the dust of the earth, water of the sea, fire of the sun and breathe of life from God and air, we receive life.

I have also used homeopathic's for many years, which reset and revive frequencies, clear out negative energies spinning with our electrons, and rewind and put the electrons in the proper orbits. The pineal gland and pituitary gland work hand-in-hand anatomically, the midbrain lies just below the pineal gland and the thalamus and hypothalamus (which hold the set points for our body for our weight, mood, temperature, metabolism, hormonal and sexual function, as well as our heart and immune function) lie in-between, just above the pituitary gland,.

I use intent to set my set points that we desire my body to have.

I started to practice pineal and pituitary toning about a year ago when the comet Elinin passed between the earth and sun on Sept 26th, 2011. I downloaded extremely high pitched frequencies into my spiritual, astral, and mental bodies, to cut off scar tissue and blockages to these critically important pineal and pituitary glands and other organs. This has been very helpful, for rejuvenating the mid-brain and glands of my clients.

Storytime:

Vicki and I traveled to Israel and Egypt about four years ago. The trip was amazing and life changing. When we were in Egypt we had the opportunity to go to the great pyramid in Giza, which was magnificent but dilapidated. Huge stones have been borrowed to build nearby homes, but the basic structure was still intact.

We went down into the king's chamber of the great pyramid, and I started toning, singing God sound vowels with such energies as ohm, ong, ahw, aeiou. The energy was amplified within the chamber and everyone in the chamber joined in with the toning. Powerful energies from the heavens entered into our bodies through the pyramid itself.

We came running out of the pyramid feeling this wonderful healing energy. I felt so good that I ran back to a woman who had stayed in the bus because she felt sick. She couldn't even get out of the bus because she had so little strength. I asked her if she wanted me to give her some energy, so she could go see the pyramid. She nodded and I said, "I see you in the pyramid."

My intuition said to touch her third eye in the middle of her forehead with my hand. Immediately I felt a surge of energy go into her third eye from my hand and it lit up her entire body. It was amazing. She suddenly stood up, climbed out of the bus, walked briskly over to the great pyramid, and went down into the entrance on the south side. When she returned with a big smile on her face, she climbed back into the bus, looking vigorous, full of life and energy. She walked straight to where I was sitting and thanked me for giving her the energy to do something she'd wanted to do for 40 years. The pyramid and her intent had reset her body to heal.

Today I Remove Virus from My Body

Various viruses create chronic dis-ease, get into our systems when our immune system is weak. They vibrate lower emotionally than all the other creatures of the planet. They need us to survive. They are expressions of guilt, blame, despair, shame and humiliation. They come in through the eyes, ears, mouth, and nose. Other orifices, such as the penis, urethra, and vagina, which normally would not be used as entrée points, can become infected. Viruses cause cancer, irritations, warts, eruptions, which our immune system if working correctly, would be quickly disposed of.

When I started medical school in the early 80's, about 5% of the people in the country had a chronic autoimmune illness. Today, there are estimates that 60% of the people have a chronic autoimmune disease, and 33% have more two or more. Petrochemicals, toxins, heavy metals and pollutants have infected our planet. Cancer is at an all time high. The medical establishment doesn't have answers to these problems, but instead is covering up the symptoms with pharmaceuticals. The answers lie in taking back your health.

Viruses are difficult to remove without changing our emotions. Forgiveness of 'self' is paramount in removing viruses from our system. Being grateful for life and the wonders of the planet is also of crucial importance. Removing guilt, blame, shame, grief, and replacing these low vibrating emotions with gratitude, self-acceptance, joy, peace, happiness, reverence, and optimism, make it difficult for viruses to survive.

Storytime:

Twenty-six years ago, when I was practicing as an OB/GYN, I noticed that many of the women in my practice were developing autoimmune diseases. New vaginal viruses transmitted sexually, were causing cervical and uterine cancers. Babies were being borne more frequently with viruses being enclosed the neural tube, causing sharp increases in attention deficit disorder (ADD), attention deficit hyperactivity disorder (ADHD) or a combination of both. Autism and Asberger's syndrome started appearing more frequently. Other poorly defined illnesses and problems with children and their mental states started increasing. In the past few years, Adult onset diabetes, chronic inflammatory illnesses and diseases and cancer in unparallel rates are showing up in families all over the world in both adults and children.

When I started medical school, breast cancer occurred in one out of twenty-five women. Now it's one in five or even more frequent. I believe it will stay at this level until we take back our health.

How do we treat viruses?

Viruses can hide in parasites, fungus, and bacteria. So, we should rid our bodies of parasites fungus and bacteria to get rid of the hiding places where virus can reinfect us. (If you turned to this part of the book, we should lower your 'viral load' by starting antiviral herbal medications formulas developed to help remove viruses from our body).

Homeopathic's are also very effective means for removing viruses.

Partners should also be treated, and if you kiss your children on the mouth, they too should be treated.

Many herbal companies have created amazing antifungal, antiviral, antibacterial, and parasite cleansing products.

I will give some examples from two companies which produce excellent products. As with any herbal regime I am supposed to tell you to consult your physician before trying them, but you are taking back control of your health and not giving it to a corporation. Corporations advertise with happy smiling people who appear sad prior to taking their products and happy after taking their products. During the commercial they will state some of the most important side effects which most people laugh at, and take the drugs anyway, because of the feeling happiness the commercials suggest.

This book will help you be a happy smiling person without all the side effects. Now, I have to tell you that these are the opinions of the author, and have not been proven in double-blind studies. Anecdotal evidence from using the products for twenty-five years, has shown amazing healing results.

Viruses, require about one month of treatment with herbs for every year the person has had the virus in their system. So if you've had a chronic viral illness, chronic autoimmune illness, or psychiatric viral illness, for five years, treatment with anti-virals for five months, if you're 22 and have had virus since you were born, it will take almost 2 years to rid the virus from your body. I have found spiritual healing and forgiveness of negative emotions of these diseases produces much quicker results. Companions, spouses, family members and friends who cause emotional distress should be dealt with, told to stop the creation of negativity. Sometimes measures to disassociate from the emotional preditors provides healing.

Practitioners of Rei Kei, emotional clearing, NAET, and other modalities can assist in clearing negative emotions to remove viruses quicker.

I call my health practitioner today for anti-viral herbs.

Storytime:

Two years ago, a woman slowly entered the office, painfully moving toward the front desk. Since I sensed her pain, I quickly crossed the room to greet her.

She stated she had been in pain since the birth of her second child, three years ago. There had been no support from the spouse of the pregnancy, and the infant had died from SIDS.

After the death of the baby, she developed severe Rheumatoid Arthritis Her doctors had treated her with anti-inflammatories, steroids, and the newer infusion pharmaceuticals, without getting relief.

Her husband had left her, unable to deal with her disease.

Intuitively, I sensed her viral load was causing her inflammation and pain. Her liver and kidneys had been compromised with the treatments up to this point in time. She started seeing a NAET practitioner and massage therapist, both helping her forgive and remove negative thoughts and emotions

We started her on anti-viral herbs, supporting her liver, kidneys and adrenals. Within two days her pain and swelling decreased by 50% and mentally she improved quickly. Three months later, her arthritis gone, life was good again.

TODAY I HELP SOMEONE ELSE HEAL

Today I will heal myself by helping another human being heal. I am stronger when I become one with another human, and sending healing energy to another person helps me become one with them. Just as the prayers of two or more people are much more powerful than a single person's prayers , healing with two or more is also much more powerful. Jesus said, "When two or more of you are gathered in my name, whatever you say will be done." Even if the intent is for me to heal the other person, the other person is also expressing his/her faith by allowing the healing to take place.

This is a very important concept, one that I have used for almost 30 years.

Katherine Beck taught me to hold a person by the hand, and with my other hand to hold the elbow of the person with the intent to channel energy for the healing. Like the center of the chest, the center of the palm, is a another center for the heart chakra. The elbow is a reception area for energy from the universe. The heart chakra already knows what the body needs to heal, and the elbow is ready to receive. As you do this, you'll feel a tingling in the hand holding the elbow, and sometimes in the palm also. Ask the beings of light, energy healers of unconditional Love, Jesus and other Masters to come and assist you in the healing.

Just remember: "If I don't do it, who will?"

Storytime:

When Vicki and I were in Israel five years ago, part of the schedule included to go to the river Jordan, to assist with baptism in the water. Carolyn Myss appointed Angela Mandato (Vicki's sister), Vicki and myself to assist in the baptisms. There were 230 people in the group, and 70 decided to be baptized. We went into a facility built at the location where Jesus is said to have been baptized, changed our clothes into white pants and shirts, and proceeded down into the Jordan River. One by one, as the people came and were baptized, we channeled the words to heal and purify them with strength and vitality. One woman who I had just baptized, as I brought her up out of the water, starred up, looking into the sky and called out, "I see Jesus". I looked up and also saw the masterful being that I'd seen about seven years earlier. We could hear angels rejoicing and singing. The energy was so delightful that many people who were not even in our group decided to join, and asked if we would baptize them. Dozens of the people in our group who had not desired to be baptized, also changed their minds, decided to have it performed for them. It was such an amazing day, all of us were enriched and filled with gratitude.

TODAY I DO SOMETHING FOR NATURE.

I will go out and say I love you to a plant, a tree, or an animal (it can be your pet), anything out in nature. Today I will bless the planet in my own small way. While I'm dictating this, a cockroach, one of my least favorite insects, ("cancel that"), came flying into my field of energy and caught my attention. She was hurt and landed upside down on the ground beside me and couldn't get up. I turned it over, my intent to heal her and it flew off. God is always trying to teach me Gratitude and thank goodness, sometimes I pay attention

My intent with this book is to help all of us to be aware of our thought. Set the intent, awareness and have mindfulness of all. In this way, healing/ restoring/ strengthening of the body can occur. It is my day to go out and strengthen, clean and purify something in my universe, which is my planet Earth and all who dwell on her..

Storytime:

One night I was out walking my dog as I frequently do, and I got to an area that we went to every night where there was a walking path down in the wash off the main roads , I enjoy walking down in that area because it is quiet and allows me to clear my head and reconnect with nature . In front of me appeared this round, glowing, cloudy, bubble, which started to coalesce into a sphere, like an orb you see in digital pictures. It started getting bigger about the size of a basketball and then coalesced into a clear golden sphere. Within it was a female fairy in a blue dress

This sort of startled me and I looked at the orb and I wondered where it could have possibly come from. The fairy within the orb glistened and shined, and all the sudden in my mind I heard the words' thank you'. As I heard the words 'thank you' I thought, "Why are you thanking me"? Then as I thought about what was going on, the little creature said, "Thank you for wanting to clean up the earth".

I thought, "Well I'm not doing much". The little fairy within the orb said, "You will have a very sick man come to you to be healed". "He will be the one who helps clean up the planet". We cannot live in your atmosphere, drink your water, or eat the food with all the pollution that is within the earth at this current time". She continued, "We used to live in this world, we called it ours, and we were able to freely move around without the protection of these orbs". "We now use this energetic force field in order to protect ourselves from this planet". "We're very sensitive to pollution and it damages our bodies and our organs within us". "The Earth used to be very clean, the water pure, the food excellent and the air breathable". "Now, we live in another realm, which is more suitable, but will return to the earth when it is purified".. I asked, "What am I supposed to do"? The answer came to my mind. I needed to continue on my path and I will eventually help creators of devices which will clean and purify our earth. I told the fairy in the orb, "Thank you very much for coming. I then asked, "What is your name"? She answered, "Aristar". She was very beautiful to look at, mesmerizing, especially the beauty of her wings.

The ferry in the orb, Aristar told me again to be watching for a man with dark hair, physically fit body, but darkness surrounding him. Dark wizards had cast spells surrounding him with cords of energy, which were suffocating him.

Then the orb slowly dissolved into the night. The whole time, my dog Angel, was looking up, very curious about the angel within the orb. It was very fascinating to see this happen that I wondered if I was just seeing things. But I was totally sober and aware, as I was out walking my dog when this curious thing happened.

This happened back in April of 2008. The next visitation occurred the next month. As one orb appeared, another two lit up the night sky. The were were equidistant from each other and appeared in a wide-ish fashion as before cloudy and then eventually cleared to reveal a golden invisible force field around three small faeries. Again the fairy said thank you. As I pondered again I wonder why they were thanking me when I hadn't really done anything. I asked them what am I doing with your thanking me for. The initial fairy Arista who have been in the initial visitation spoke and said quotation mark you are helping heal the humans. By doing this you will help heal the planet. As you teach them to heal their bodies they will become more aware of all of the animals and creatures of this planet and become more consistent in trying to be environmentally friendly. As you help them raise their frequency and love themselves they will start loving everything around them the us you will help save the planet. You will also see a man who will come to you who is developing an end environmentally correct way of cleaning up waste and recycling products. He has already started building his factory but he will become sec and you will see him and take care of him. He will be a key instrument in helping clean up the earth and the oceans of the earth. You will be the key in helping him stay strong and healthy so he can complete his task. Through this you will be a great source of help in cleaning up the planet by helping others stay healthy and strong and thus, they will go on and clean up the planet. I was fascinated by this talk of me helping others to help the planet. I've always believed that my true duty was to help others be healthier but I didn't realize this would help the planet be healthier. To your started dancing and going in a circular fashion. They started dating away and as they faded away I heard that Bob thank you again and so I said in my mind no thank you for coming and giving me this message of inspiration. The entire time that this was happening Angel was looking directly up your media tell she was saying something them to them and talking to them at the same time. I often wonder if dogs don't communicate much better telepathically than we do. We continued our walk and were greatly inspired due to this visitation of the orb's. I believe that all orbs are faeries or creatures from other realms who have had to surround themselves in a force field to protect them from our environment talk our environmental toxins.

Since the time of the experience of the fairies, a man came into my office, who was quite ill due to negative energies trying to destroy his life. We cleared these energies and are currently helping him detoxify his body and become healthier through homeopathic remedies, herbs and encouragement and teaching him how to protect himself from these negative entities.

The man who came to my office also had built an environmentally friendly recycling plant which was totally enclosed and recycled everything including the water it used in the recycling efforts. I am very grateful to have been included in helping his life. He is a visionary engineer who has dreams of designing, the brings into reality environmentally important facilities cleaning up our world.

As I continue my life and continue to do the work which spirit has given me to do, I'm very grateful for all the people who come into my life, including fairies who have encouraged me to continue on my path.

TODAY I LEARN A NEW TECHNIQUE FOR BREATHING AND MEDITATION

I take a deep breath, hold it very deep for 10 seconds, and then breathe out, releasing all of my feelings and desires to the universe.

I take another deep breath, and I visualize a small pinpoint of light in front of my third eye . I exhale, thanking the energy for coming.

I then inhale deeply until the pinpoint of light enters into my third eye, expanding into the optic chiasm, behind my eyes and into my pituitary gland. I then breathe out.

I take in another breath taking another pinpoint of light into my third eye and back into the my pituitary gland expanding the energy and perfecting it. Then I breathe out.

Next I breathe a pinpoint of light through my cerebral chakra on top of my head into the pineal gland. The light hits my pineal gland and lights it up with energy. I then breathe out.

I inhale, visualizing a pinpoint of light at the back of my head, which enters in at the occipital prominence (small bone sticking out midway between the top of the head and the neck) and the light expands into the occipital lobe of my brain where sight and hearing are processed. This lights up the occipital lobe of my brain and the energy expands and perfects my brain consciousness of light and sound. Then I exhale out.

I then visualize two points of perfect light from source energy outside the ears. Breathing in these points of light, which enter into my ears on both sides of my head, expanding into the middle ear, then expanding into the inner ear, the semicircular canals and then into the auditory complex, perfecting these tissues and expanding into the brain. I then breathe out.

I then visualize two small points of light and breathe them in through both nostrils, then into the olfactory bulb and complex. The light enters the nervous system bringing the points of light into the midbrain and pons, lighting up this portion of the brain, and then back into the olfactory complex of nerves. I then breathe out.

I visualize a small point of light in front of my mouth. As I inhale the light enters in the center of my tongue and spreads throughout the taste buds of my tongue. I place my tongue on the roof of my mouth, and I send the energy into the tasting center within my brain, which lights up with energy and perfection. I then breathe out.

I take in another breath bringing a pinpoint of light in the mouth, touching the roof of my mouth with my tongue moving the light up. I then roll my eyes up bringing the pinpoint of light into the frontal cortex which now creates a complete energetic circle within my brain, including the sides of my brain. I then breathe out.

I will practice this breathing exercise each morning for the next week. This technique is specific for energizing and helping the auditory, olfactory, taste buds and centers, and visual parts of the brain, including the sensatory regions of the cerebral cortex

Storytime:

I was teaching a class on breathing when the above breathing technique described above, was channeled to me. It was interesting to learn that many other practitioners teaching the same type of breathing. People are channeling the same types of techniques all over the world.

In this class, I was teaching everybody to heal with this energy expanding within the brain and energizing and perfecting the brain. As a group, you could feel all of our energy merging, creating this beautiful unconditional love.

I was then inspired to teach the students, a visualization of a small pinpoint in the heart, which we continued expanding to the point until we filled the United States with the light and love, with peace and order, joy and happiness, love and gratitude.

After we completed the exercise filling the universe with our love gratitude, I sensed that everyone in the room was in a place of a higher vibration. I also sensed that our city was more peaceful and at a higher vibration. I sensed that our state was at a higher vibration and also the entire nation. Somehow one little group of 12 people made a huge change in our universe, which made complete sense to me. We are all one, and what a few of us do, affects the whole.

That night I went to sleep knowing we had assisted the universe to be more peaceful. I understood what it meant to expand the energies throughout our universe. The next day many of the people called and reported how peaceful their night had been and how peaceful their families felt, but then, the whole day how peaceful all the people we met during the day had been.

With this breathing exercise, you will sleep better tonight, your family will sleep better and the whole world will sleep better, thanks to your participation.

TODAY I WILL DO A REGRESSION THERAPY GOING INTO MY PAST TO CLEAR ENERGIES THAT ARE NOT SERVING ME OR MY HIGHEST GOOD.

Today I will find a regression therapist.

I will access past emotional, physical, mental and spiritual experiences which are keeping me from moving forward in my evolution.

A light hypnotic state, assisted by my therapist, will correct and release energies that are keeping me from healing.

Storytime:

Several years ago my wife Vicki studied regression therapy to clear emotions from present and past experiences. She studied with Brian Weiss, M.D. and Dolores Cannon whom have written several books on the subject. What is Regression therapy? A technique for guided meditation and light hypnosis, allowing the subconscious mind to go back into your past, to heal the present. You go to this place with the intent of clearing any energies which are not for your highest good. Often, at the time of conception, our growth within the womb, our childhood, adolescence, early adult life or our past life experiences have injured us. This can cause deep wounds, that are carried into the present.

There were many instances which stay with us, our entire life, and we are not quite sure what they are, but they don't allow us progress, they hold us back from being all we can be.

Here is a regression technique you can use right now. Lie down in a quiet and comfortable place, using a pillow if possible.

Take a breath to clear your energy. Clear all your thoughts and go into a place of peace and happiness. Exhale, then breathe in again visualizing yourself being on a cloud, of beautiful love, which takes you up to the sky. The cloud takes you to the place and time that needs to be healed. Then breathe out

Visualize the fluffy cloud descending slowly and gently to the ground. Look around and see where you are. See, smell, feel and touch every thing around you. Then, breathe out.

Look at your feet. What are you wearing on them? Are they bare, without shoes or socks? How does the ground feel underneath your feet? Focus on the feelings you are feeling, smell the air around you, sense what you see and hear.

Look around you and see if there is anyone you know.

If so, approach them, tell them you love them, show your gratitude and thankfulness for their soul, with whatever you feel at this moment, tell them you're sorry you have to go and you ask for forgiveness for anything that may have happened between you, that may have harmed either one of you. You talk to them resolving any other issues and again express your gratitude, gratefulness and love, thanking them for their time.

Look at your body. See the love, that is a gift from God. It is perfect, grateful, more happy and joyous. You have healed. The loving person that you healed, healed you, too. Both of you feel differently. Not only did you heal yourself, but you healed them through your love. You bring that love and that feeling of healing, forward to this present moment in time. Open your eyes, sense the love of the light in the clearing of the old energy. Any negative energy no longer exists, there is a new paradigm and time line for both your souls.

Storytime:

Vicki and I use this technique quite frequently. By going into more depth, we can heal many emotions and events during one session. In my last session we went back to when I was conceived in the womb. My mother hadn't wanted to become pregnant, because my older sister being only 5 months old. My dad was in the military and was gone a lot. He was having an affair, and her intuition let her know this was happening. She did not want to be pregnant and have an absent father for the baby. During the pregnancy my mom asked for a divorce and moved back with her parents. I have two older siblings which came in wanted and loved my mother, but she struggled during her entire pregnancy with me.

As a fertilized egg and as I grew into an embryo, I struggled to be alive. Unwanted, un- loved, I just desired to be alive. I was born, a very sickly child. Multiple times during my first year, the doctors and my mother wondered if I would live through the infections and illnesses that I constantly had. During the regression session, I visualized my dad loving my mother and their their getting along well. They were divorced, but they loved me, wanted me and were grateful for me. My whole body shook, during the session, several times with the changes taking place through dimensions of space, time, and thought.

Vicki and I brought this new timeline and paradigm forward to the present. when we did the regression, which was actually only a few months ago. I have felt very different toward my father and my mother ever since that regression.

My father had died two years ago and I made peace with him since that moment. My father did the best he could with the knowledge he had. Now there was a forgiveness of love and compassion that helped both of us heal. My mother has felt more loving towards me, also. She feels changed and happy to me. She asked me how I'm doing and I tell her, "Mom, I love you".

TODAY I CUT THE CORDS OF ENERGETIC DRAINAGE AND PROTECT MYSELF FROM ANY NEGATIVE ATTACHMENTS

As I go through life, I have negative and positive attachments to others. Today, I'm cutting off all the negative attachments.

I take a deep breath and clear my mind. I set my intent to let go of my negative attachments, I then exhale.

I then take a deep grounding breath, grounding myself deep into the earth. I then Exhale.

Next, I inhale deep breath connecting to the heavens-- connecting to source energy -- bringing that energy down into my body. I then exhale.

I visualize a flaming sword, with a long blade, that I move easily in my hand. This is the flaming sword of truth that I'm going to use to cut off all the negative attachments. These attachments to my energetic body appear as cords of light coming out my spiritual body, my emotional body, and my mental body. Negative cords drain my body's energy. These are the cords that I will cut and detach. They are connected energectically to my body, to my neck, to my head, to my arms and hands, legs and feet.

With the flaming sword, I cut all these attachments, around my head, my back, my arms and hands, my legs and feet, and my entire body. I cut any and all negative attachments especially to my creative chakra and root chakra. Be sure to cut behind your back all the way up your spine and all down the back, in between my legs, I bring the blade round the side of each leg bring it up through the groin area, slicing off any negative attachments bringing the sword up around the back, up around my neck and around my head completely encircyling it, cutting off all negative attachments. When I am done, I take all of these cords of energy, which were attached to me, take them in my hands, with intent to receive their energy source from the source where they should have been receiving it. All of these attachments are no longer sucking energy from me, but they are receiving their energy from the source.

Now I put a sphere of silver light around me with the intent for silver shield to bounce off any negative energies that aren't for my best and highest good. I breathe in again, visualizing a golden sphere around the outside of the silver sphere with the intent to protect my energy and only allow good energies to enter into my aura. This golden sphere, will also bounce off any negative energies attempting to enter my field of energy. I then visualize a violet flame of God's energy outside of the golden sphere. The purpose of this violet flame is to transmute any energies coming towards me or which have been bounced off by this silver or golden spheres which are not for my best and highest good. The violet flame transmutes negative energies, changing these energies into an energy which will become good and won't harm anyone else.

All these shields will protect me from people, entities, aliens, demons or other negative energies that have been draining my energy and will protect me from them reattaching.

All I need to do is say, "Shields up," with the intent to have this protection all day. If you sence someone is sucking out your energy, just say, "Shields up" aloud or just in your thought.

So be it!

Story time:

About 15 years ago, I was involved in transforming my energetic vibration and raising my energy to a higher state. My wife at the time seemed constantly angry at me because she thought, I didn't understand her or vibrate with her or her family's energy. I would not join in her heated conversations; in fact I quit attending her family dinners because they were always picking on someone in the family. My ex-wife's brother and sister-in-law had raised their vibrations energetically and actually left the family. They became the brunt of every negative Sunday dinner conversation, when in actuality, the rest of the family were all very sad without these two higher vibrating beings and their children.

When I stopped going to the dinners, I explained why I was not coming. "I can't be around the hurtful words and thoughts being created." "I desire to be surrounded by higher vibrating beings so I keep my own vibration higher".

A couple of years later, I met my present wife, Vicki. I felt like I had come home. Her sister, Angela, a shaman, performed a ritual in which we cleared negative attachments using an actual sword. Each one of us would step into a fire pit, where one at a time, we underwent a ritual of cutting off negative attachments. We would stand in the middle of a fire and took the sword in our hands, cutting off all the negative attachments.

I remember the air being sucked out of my lungs. I was gasping for the air. It felt like the flames were sucking the life right out of me. I knew I didn't have a lot of time. I selected the negative attachments on my body and as quickly as possible I cut them off. I couldn't take it anymore. I was about to pass out, when all of a sudden, I received a beam of radiant energy from within my chest and I started breathing again. I stepped away from the fire and saw that my feet had black soot on them, but they didn't hurt. Instead of being burnt, my body felt radiant. My soul felt at peace and 100% perfect. My energy was sealed up from any attachments.

I don't need to stand in the fire, but using a flaming sword to cut off the attachments is very effective. Whenever I feel negative attachments, I imagine a flaming sword cutting the attachments from my body so that they no longer suck out my energy. I surround myself with silver and gold spheres, with the violet flame of God to transmute negative energy into good positive energy, which protects others from being picking up the negative energy.

Today I will protect myself from any negative attachments.

TODAY I WILL BE READY WHEN THE TEACHER COMES.

Today I will allow that person to be my teacher.

Many times I ask for an answer from God. The answers, often come in the form of people who just happen to show up in my life. They may seem intrusive, they intrude on me, my way of life and my way of doing things, but they are here to teach me the lessons that the universe/God wants me to know.

Today I will raise my frequency and be open to the messages that the Universe/God is telling me.

I am open and receptive.

Today I will be open to receiving a messenger from the Universe/ God who comes into my life.

I will embrace them and will stop what I am doing and will bring them in and listen to their message for my life.

When Jesus was upon the earth, the apostles asked the question," How can we recognize God?" Jesus then said to the disciples, " If I was hungry you fed me, if I was naked, you gave me clothes, if I was cold you gave me warmth." Jesus continued on about how every person we meet is the Christ. We need to take care of each other, love each other, be kind to each other, take care of each other's needs.

Today I accept the messenger of God sent to me.

Storytime:

I arrived in Maui the second week in the Hawaiian islands, being sent by my wife to help a woman she had met at the Grammy Awards in Hollywood, who had been diagnosed with fibromyalgia/chronic fatigue syndrome. Maui was not a part of my plan, but something inside me told me I should go.

Flying into this beautiful healing Island was wonderful. This beautiful angel by the name of Mary Langston, picked me up in a van filled with all the wonderful things in her life helping her live in Maui.

She was so happy because the day before, she was feeling very sick, and very depressed. She had asked me to help her and over the phone I had sent her some toning energy (God sounds) to energize her system. Within 15 minutes, her body and mental state totally changed for the better. She couldn't stop talking about how grateful she was to be feeling better. The house she was staying in was on the slope of the volcano above the waters and she felt so good she wanted to go to the ocean, to go swimming. And after we gave her the energy that she traveled (walked two miles) down to the ocean. There were no dolphins or whales to be found, but still her energy was so good that she wanted to meet me the next day to see who this person was, that sent energy through the etheric and astral planes, energy directly for her body.

As we talked, we discussed a person by the name of Matthew, who goes into the void and brings messages out from the void. The void is nowhere, yet everywhere, the place (for a better description) where creation begins; it's where our universe was brought into being.

Matthew at the age of 18, was riding his bike, and he came to a point on the trail, where he could go left on the trail, which would've taken him over a cliff or he could go right, which would bring him safely home. A voice came into his head and told him to take the right turn.

Mary had come to Maui to follow and listen to the teachings of Matthew.

This happy soul (Mary), picked me up at the airport, and out of gratitude, she brought me to where I was supposed to stay. She was so gracious and helpful and kind. She helped me to understand that Matthew is a messenger, teaching from the void. His message from God to us.

As I watched YouTube's of Matthew, he spoke very slowly and methodically with very inspiring words and energy. I had the sense that he had important messages from the powers of creation, messages of love from the void.

We are always where we are supposed to be, however, not always receptive. We are not always in the vibration we are supposed to be in. To receive the message, a radio must be tuned to the right frequency. When we are at the right frequency and open to receive an even higher frequency, we will receive the message.

TODAY I WILL SOAK MY FEET IN A FOOT BATH WITH MAGNESIUM AND/OR BATH SALTS

One of the kindest things I can do for myself, is to take care of my feet. Magnesium sulfate or Epson salts is very beneficial for this. There is a machine called the BEFE machine or bioelectric Field Enhancement ionic generating device, that has an array that I place in salted water, which passes a gentle direct current of electricity. My feet are then put into big plastic dish pan of warm salt (Epsom salts are preferred) water (a gallon or two of water). Once it is the temperature I desire, place your feet into a dishpan or a bucket that is large enough to be comfortable. If you do not have one of these frequency generating devices, just put half of a cup of magnesium sulfate or bath salts into the bucket of water. Feet should be in the water/salt mixture and soak for 30 minutes.

My feet take me where I desire to go
My feet move me through this life. My feet often get neglected.

We cut our hair and comb or brush it daily, trim our finger nails at least weekly. We change our clothes and wash our bodies daily, but often our feet get neglected.

Today I will love and take care of my feet.

Storytime:

Ten years ago at my office in Cedar City we had a seminar, taught by Fawn, one of the massage therapists, who worked out of the office. The seminar was about Reflexology. It was an excellent "hand's on" Seminar. An older women who was attending, was having great difficulty walking. Each step was carefully placed and painful. I noticed that her feet had huge cracks and the souls were thickened and cracked, with flakes of fungus attached along the sides and bottoms. At the end of the seminar, I asked her, if she would like me to help her feet feel better by doing a foot bath and rub them down afterward with oil.

This woman agreed and consented to take thirty minutes out of her life and allow someone to care for her. We warmed the water and placed it in a bucket and added some Epsom salts, and we had the benefit of using a bioelectrical frequency generating device. We put the array in the water, turned on the machine and soaked her feet in the water for 30 minutes.

As the electrical current passes through the water, it ionizes the water into hydrogen and hydroxyl ions. These ions open up the pores in the feet releasing toxins into the water. The magnesium salts softens the hardened cracks of the skin. The cracked and hardened tissue is more easily removed after the soaking and by using the ionic device.

At the end of the session, the top of the water had white material floating with some black specks. The water underneath was brownish-yellow. I removed her feet, and dried them off with a paper towel, which became brownish yellow from the residue on her feet. I rubbed and rubbed her feet to remove the dead tissue caused by the fungus.

The magnesium sulfate had softened the tissues, helped to bring relief to her feet, as magnesium allows for more circulation. I took Olive Oil and rubbed it into her feet. While I massaged the olive oil into the cracks and tissues of her feet and in between her toes, she stated, "This is the kindest thing another human being has ever done for me." Her feet had been dirty and the soaking cleansed the feet and restored her feet so they had quit hurting. The olive oil lubricated and absorbed into the dry skin making the skin softer. When I had finished, I noticed that she had been crying. She told me that her feet had been hurting her for years. She was over 50 years old.

Today I will be kind to my feet, love and thank them for taking me where I need to go in this life.

TODAY I WILL TAKE CARE OF MY BODY BY SEEING A REFLEXOLOGIST

Reflexology is the study of different points on the bottoms and sides of the feet and ankles, which are associated with the different organs and systems of the body. Reflexologists have studied these points and scientifically mapped out the energetic associations. The foot is a representation of different parts of the body including the brain, central nervous system and the spine. Our bodies are amazing in that each part of the body is associated with other parts of the body, the organs and organ systems. The toes represent different parts of the brain and cranial nerves. The glands in the brain are in the big toe, the pineal and pituitary glands. The different organs and systems are found throughout the foot and in the sole of the foot.

Today I allow a professional reflexologist to take care of my feet.

Storytime:

I was flying to Phoenix, Arizona, to travel to Scottsdale to give lectures on alternative healing methods, and to make appointments for intuitive medical spiritual readings about two years ago. I had noticed a ball of tissue developing in the flexor tendon of my left foot. I desired to see a reflexologist. By intuition, I chose to go to a particular business which had both a massage therapist and a reflexologist.

As the reflexologist examined my feet , he found the hard ball of tissue. He asked me how long it had been there. I wasn't sure, but it had been a few months. He wasn't sure exactly what was causing the hardened tissue, but felt it was probably the pancreas and/or the liver. I intuitively felt it was the pancreas and had him rub it especially hard to loosen up the tissue and breakup whatever was going on in my pancreas.

But, I wasn't vigilant about continuing the therapy.

A year and a half later I ended up, having a problem with my pancreas. My pancreas and liver had caused me a great deal of pain in my feet very early on, showing me where the problem would be in the future.

I believe if I had continued the therapy on my feet, my pancreas would've never been compromised.

Part of the healing is allowing different healers to take care of you. It costs money and it takes time, but in the long run, they'll take good care of your body and help you to feel better. The money you pay for these healers, will be money well spent.

TODAY I WILL EAT FRESH ORGANIC PAPAYA, PASSION FRUIT, AND/OR PINEAPPLE.

Today, I will eat fresh passion fruit, pineapple and/or papaya which break up **diseased** tissue. The natural enzymes breakdown mucus within the body that may be surrounding tumors, gall or kidney stones, parasites or other problems in my body. Eating fresh fruit, especially these three, is very beneficial for the dissolving and removing mucus and cellular membranes surrounding parasites. It can also help to dissolve stones in the liver, pancreas, gallbladder and kidneys. Buying the freshest fruit you can find or pick it off the tree. I would recommend one organic papaya, two organic passion fruit and half an organic pineapple twice a day. A pineapple is too large to eat the whole thing in one sitting, but you can eat it throughout the day. Drink lots of water while you do this. At least a gallon throughout the day. The fresher fruit has more enzymes. This is a different sort of cleanse which is excellent for your liver, pancreas, gallbladder and kidneys.

And storytime:

I awoke in the middle of the night with severe abdominal pain, like a knife stabbing and twisting just below my stomach. I knew it was my pancreas. There was large stone trapped in the ampulla of Vater, the distal hepatopancreatic duct, where the pancreatic juices (pancreatic enzymes) and bile dump into the duodenum to digest food. This duct from the pancreas was blocked with a stone. The pain became quite excruciating, and I woke up knowing I had to either go to the hospital or the big Island of Hawaii, because the volcano there and fresh fruit would help me to heal.

I nudged Vicki to wake her up and stated, "We need to go to the Big Island Hawaii." She told me that we could make plans to go in a couple months for our anniversary. I said, "No, I need to go today or tomorrow."

That morning, Vicki's sister, Barbara, came over her to the house, with her boyfriend to eat breakfast. Barbara told Vicki they were leaving to go to the Big Island Hawaii, with six people total were going, because they had six tickets that had been given to her. Vicki asked if she could get two more tickets. Barbara wasn't sure, because the friend who had gotten the tickets only had six -- but she said she would call him up.

Providence intervened. Barbara called her friend, and her friends boss had just given him two extra tickets that morning. She asked if she could have them, and he said yes, and she screamed and screamed with delight, telling Vicki, that we were all going to Kona together. The eight of us drove down to Los Angeles the next day, to the LAX airport, boarded a plane and we were off to Kona, on the Big Island of Hawaii.

When we arrived at the airport in Hawaii, I knew I needed to get some fresh papaya and passion fruit. We rented two cars and started to drive south, through Kona and around the southern area of the island. One of the people with us, knew the island well, and many people in the Kona, Hawaii area.

The first house we stopped at had fresh papaya ready for picking. Fresh pineapple was also available and we start eating our breakfast.

Immediately I felt the stone in my duct start to soften. Fresh papaya was plentiful and passion fruit was also picked and eaten. Butter avocados were falling off the trees and added to the delight of the breakfast. As I ate these fresh fruits, my pain subsided but was still present.

We headed up to the volcano and went down into the caldera or cooking pot, a cauldron-like Volcanic feature usually formed by the collapse of land following a volcanic eruption. I was told intuitively that toning, (sounds of creation, from the universe using the vocal cords) and using energy coming off of the volcano in the caldera, would dissolve and pass the stone in my pancreas. The stone was still present, but had been softened by the papaya, pineapple and passion fruit. Vicki,

Syndi (Vicki's twin sister), Shariel (Vicki's mother), Barbara (Vicki's sister) and Lex (Now Barbara's husband) hiked with me, down into the Caldera of Kilauea, at Volcanoes National Park.

Hiking down, we arrived in the bottom of the caldera, which seems like the surface of the moon except darker. I started with an "Om", toning at the note F above middle C. All six of us joined in with the sounds. We then toned a middle C. with an "ong," using our voices together, to creat a dome of energy within the caldera. We continued our toning, with different God sounds, when with great relief, I felt the stone pass through my pancreatic duct.

Such sweetness and joy filled my soul as the stone passed. Shariel (Vicki's mother), who had also been having abdominal pain for six months, was relieved of her pain when we did the toning.

If I had gone to the hospital, the pancreatitis would have been treated by keeping me off food, putting IVs in me, and possibly ending up with a Whipple procedure. In the Whipple operation the head of the pancreas, a portion of the bile duct, the gallbladder and the duodenum are removed. Occasionally a portion of the stomach may also be removed as they all have the same blood supply.

In pancreatitis, the pancreas is eaten by the enzymes that it produces. As the pancreatitis worsens and continues (chronic pancreatitis), it releases even more Enzymes, which causes the pancreas is to swell and die. The tissues surrounding the pancreas can also become diseased and swollen. The **islets of Langerhans** are the regions of the pancreas that contain its endocrine (i.e., hormone-producing) cells. There are five types of cells in an islet: alpha cells that make glucagon, which raises the level of glucose (sugar) in the blood; beta cells that make insulin; **Insulin** is a hormone, produced by the pancreas, which is central to regulating carbohydrate and fat metabolism in the body. Insulin causes cells in the liver, muscle, and fat tissue to take up glucose from the blood, storing it as glycogen inside these tissues; delta cells that make somatostatin which inhibits the release of numerous other hormones in the body; and PP cells, in the head of the pancreas, the pancreatic polypeptide hormone is expressed at times when glucose levels in the blood are low. D1 cells, about which little is known. Degeneration or absence of the insulin-producing beta cells is the main cause of type I (insulin-dependent) diabetes mellitus. So people undergoing the Whipple procedure need insulin and enzymes the rest of their life to survive.

I am so grateful for my pancreas being healed and healthy.

Today, I day will take care of my body by eating fresh organic papaya, pineapple and passion fruit.

TODAY I WHISTLE A HAPPY SONG
OR MAKE MUSIC WITH A FLUTE

Today I will whistle a tune or happy song with my mouth or on a flute. Music is the voice of the gods. Music also helps me be happy. With whistling, the lips are pursed together, forming the kiss of sound as you blow out the pranic energy of the universe. It makes a "God sound," similar to toning. Some people can even make a whistling sound between their teeth and tongue coming from inside their mouth.

I learned about the power of whistling from a shaman in Peru. As the shaman was whistling, I could see the sound create waves of energy, that pushed out negative energies in the bodies and souls of those present.

The piercing energy of the whistling penetrated the deepest parts of their bodies. As the waves of energy, created an environment that negative entities could not tolerate, they would then leave the body of that individual.

Whistling is a wonderful energy. Whistling is a powerful mode of energetic conversation that tells the universe you're happy. As the shaman in the jungle whistled, it cleared negative energies and protected those doing a ceremony.

Different pitches can cause different changes within the body. All of these changes are good.

A flute can also be used if you can't whistle with your mouth.

Storytime:

Two years ago, when we were in Peru, we participated in a ceremony down in the jungle. We drank a mixture of herbs including some vine of the soul and then, lay down on our mats. The shaman began to sing to us, and then to whistle. The whistling was pure music to my ears. The whistling and songs cleared the energy around us, then entered our bodies, causing waves of purified energy to enter in, removing negative energies from our bodies.

For one woman, the whistling started helping her to remove dangerous drug residues, left inside her body, releasing the detrimental effects which had plagued her for years.

For another woman, it helped remove the negative emotions from within her body.

For myself, it stimulated me to go to spiritual levels where my questions were easily answered. The whistling and singing was a marvelous experience, one that I will never forget.

The whistling pierced through the veil, helping us to see the other side. The whistling scared off negative energies and protected us on our spiritual journey.

Today I will whistle a happy tune.

If you're unable to whistle, playing the flute will bring the same benefits.

TODAY I WILL PUT ON SOME
MUSIC AND DANCE.

Dance -- rhythmic swaying and moving of the hips, legs, feet, head and the arms. Dance is one of the most powerful methods of moving energy. It moves energy all over the body creating a vibrational energy which heals the soul. A positive vortex is created with the energetic movement. These vortices are very powerful for healing the body.

Dancing can change your life.

Dancing can heal your body.

If you don't "know how" to dance, just move your body.

The use of high vibrating music can create the energy for you. High vibrating music can move the body. It can clear the mind, clear the energy surrounding you. The rhythmic movement of dancing and flow of your body creates even more energy. The movements and flow created through dance surround your body and create good energy flow.

Have you ever wondered why you love to watch a beautiful dancer?

It's because they create and move energy and our eyes perceive the beauty and the flow of the energy. We feel the energetic movement of the energy. The sound of the music allows us to hear the vibration energy. We sense and incorporate into the body, the energy of the movement and sound.

Storytime:

My energy level was down quite severely with the pancreatitis. I had desired to move and be able to live near the ocean, I was supposed to stay in St. George, Utah.

Around Christmas time, middle of December, Vicki and I attended a dance where Vicki's brother, Richard and his band, 'Eye 15' were playing. They were playing 80's music, and the music was very uplifting good easy rock. I love to dance. My energy was quite low but the energy of the people dancing and the band, raised my own energy and I decided to dance. The movement of my body with the music invigorated and strengthened me, raising my energy level. We stayed and danced until the band was done playing around midnight.

As we drove home early Sunday morning, I was so grateful for the energy, but I had a rough time going to sleep, because I was singing the tunes in my mind all night. That morning, I awoke feeling much more energetic and integrated.

Today I will put on some music and dance!

TODAY I REACH OUT TO A FRIEND FROM THE PAST

Having a friend, outside of my primary family, relatives and inner circle, is important.

This relationship, can help me get through emotional times to help me see things by offering a different perspective.

This loving, kind, understanding, friend can be one of the most important people in my life. This is someone that I can share my weakest moments, the tough times, the rough times, who will help me get out of my emotional ruts as easily as possible.

Turning to others for emotional support or comfort, allows help to be there for me.

When I take responsibility for my feelings, I instigate the first step towards learning, growing and moving on. Responsibility includes looking for support.

An old friend, can see me from the perspective of my youth, helps me to heal my past.

Asking them for help, shows them, I am human, helps them to feel important, and they will have fond memories of me, and they will feel the happiness that I made contact with them and that I still desire them as a friend.

The problems still belong to me, however an old friend, they can help me release and see it from a different perspective.

Emotionally if you feel alone, find a friend, who you can express those emotions to safely.

Storytime:

I went through a very harsh experience ten years ago. I was angry and frustrated.

Felt like I had been badly mistreated and misunderstood.

Fortunately, the universe provided a friend for me, who offered unconditional love, a listening ear, and was nonjudgmental of what was happening. I could tell her anything without fear, without judgment, without consequence. She helped me get through the anger and feelings of self-deprecation (Disparagement or undervaluation of oneself and one's abilities).

The most crucial feelings in life, are the right to love and be loved, without judgment.

A trusted friend, can alleviate the pressure imposed on us by the world and ourselves.

Vicki met all of my needs for a perfect friend.

She trusted everything that I said to her.

She listened with an open heart.

She empathized my pain, and didn't judge me.

To meet all one's needs, a trusted friend can reduce the demands of life, help reduce the load and pressure.

The mere act of giving, growing together, inspiring, and sharing creativity of thought and mind are the keys of friendship.

To give, without expecting something in return, is the ultimate gift of love.

Good society or friendship, will do everything it can to draw out, good things in our lives.

Honor your choices and the inherent responsibility that comes with those choices.

Share the burden of those choices with a true friend.

Only then can you realize, your true potential, to give love and receive love.

TODAY I CALL IN THE ARCHANGELS TO SURROUND ME AND PROTECT ME

Today, I sit or lay down in a comfortable position, take a deep breath, then I exhale, blowing out all my troubles. With the intent to call in the archangels, I take another deep breath and say, "I call Archangel Michael in front of me, Archangel Raphael behind me, Archangel Gabriel to my right, and Archangel Ariel to my left." My intent is for them to surround me and protect me with their love and protective energy. They also clear any negative emotions, feelings or energies that might be surrounding me in my energetic field. "So be it."

Now, if there is something bothering me, I ask the archangels to protect me, teach me, and love me through the difficulty. I can also ask for other angels to remove the feelings of fear.

Storytime:

Every time I fly, it seems as if the plane gets into air turbulence. When taking off and landing, I always ask for ten legions of Angels to come and help. The minute I ask, the plane stop shaking and swerving. This always restores confidence to the pilot or copilot and all those assisting the pilots with landing and taking off.

I'm telling recent stories because they are more recent on my mind. Flying from Honolulu to Maui, the airplane was coming down into turbulence because a big storm was coming in. The wind was blowing hard. The pilot called over the intercom, "We may have a rough go of it. For your safety, fasten your safety belts." The plane was shifting, and we suddenly dropped with everone's drinks flying into the air. We were losing elevation fast. I was really concerned because sheering winds were pulling the plane up and down, to the right and left.

Immediately I asked for 20,000 angels to help calm the winds and stabilize the plane.

As soon as I projected this thought, the plane stopped shaking. Twenty legends of Angels, stabilized the wind and guided the aircraft down, giving us a very soft easy landing.

This has occurred so many times with aircraft that I no longer fear flying, I just automatically believe, ask for the Angels to help, and it is so.

TODAY AND EVERY DAY, I AM ONE WITH THE UNIVERSE. THE UNIVERSE IS ONE WITH ME. I AND THE UNIVERSE ARE ONE.

My universe is a unique and ideal location for evolution of my soul.

I, as an individual, have unique opportunities for growth that are presented to me, according to my birthday, my family and extended family I live with. The emotional environment I grow up in, my friends, and my past life connections give me situations which will assist with my karma, dharma, and all aspects of my souls growth.

Luckily, the universe is forgiving. My intent creates thoughts, and my thoughts create my thought forms, and my thought forms, create energy which affects everything and everyone around me.

When my intent is to do good, I create good. If my intent is to do something else, I do other things that may be poisonous to my own soul and the souls of others.

Karmic payback is what I accumulate when I make poor decisions. My decisions affect others in a positive or negative way. This energy can be undone by changing my intent and thoughts, and by doing good deeds.

So today I become one with the universe. By doing good, and the universe will become one with me, for good.

Storytime:

While in Maui I felt uneasiness. There was something left undone in my past that I needed to fix. It wasn't something I did in this life time, but something in another time, a long ago.

Maggie Rayne, from whom I was renting a room, was having her husband see a hypno-therapist.

I felt it would be beneficial for me to also see the hypno-therapist. So I made an appointment and went to see Gayle Barklie. I told her, "I've never been able to be hypnotized." She said, "We'll see about that". She used every technique she knew of, to put me under hypnosis, and it was actually quite a bit of fun as her worked to get me under hypnosis. When I finally did go under, I went to a place in France about 600 years ago.

I was a wizard by the name of Edmond, chief wizard to King Philip.

The King had an indiscreet love affair and I knew about it. I had used this knowledge against the King to become rich, and because of this, the king eventually had me beheaded by guillotine.

To correct this situation, we used a space and time technique in which I did not use the information of the affair against King Phillip. I was a kind and honorable wizard who lived a full life and was never beheaded. Then we brought the energy of that past life forward into the present or current life. It felt good, I felt whole, and I felt healed. As a side note, a neck pain went away that I had suffered with my whole life.

You may or may not believe in past life regression. I have had many instances where going back in time and space, and sometimes to another dimension, which helped heal old wounds and patterns which repeat themselves again and again.

This duality, this universe, is the perfect playground for my soul to experience growth. Now is the time to become one with the universe.

To do this, I say, "I am one with the universe, the universe is one with me. I and the universe are one."

TODAY I LOVE MYSELF UNCONDITIONALLY AND STOP A BAD HABIT

I may or may not be a smoker, but if I have a habit that is detrimental to my health, it's time to stop.

This book is about taking back your health. I've been told many times to stop, whatever bad habit I'm doing, for my health. I know what is bad for me. I know the habits which keep my body unhealthy.

Multiple bad habits have caused me to injure my body, such as: drinking too much alcohol, smoking cigarettes, using Marijuana for other than medicinal purposes (just to check out or get high), eating too much sugar, consuming to many chemicals that stimulate the brain, using drugs for recreation or just using drugs to try feeling better, getting in too much caffeine, watching or reading pornography, and many other habits which affect my emotional inner psyche, These habits can be carried forward from another lifetime and continued. Habits that injure this body and mind in this lifetime.

I have found one of the easiest ways to get rid of a bad habit is to go back, retrace to when and where it began, to fill the void (which caused the bad habit in the first place) with something good.

It's called retracing and reformatting, just like a computer that's gone bad. I have to go back (retrace where the problem began) and re-format (clean up the hard drive or mess I caused, by getting rid of the virus or bad information).

I change what happened, clean up my system, and bring it forward with good intent, positive thoughts to reboot a state of good health.

I may know_____ (fill in with whatever bad habit I have) is bad for me, but I continue to do it anyway -- maybe as a type of rebellion, maybe as a form of self comfort, maybe I just got addicted.

I have for years, used a this habit of _____which is harming my body, to self-justify. It just takes me making the decision to stop _____(fill in the bad habit), and then I will set my intent to quit.

I will move forward and do what it takes to stop _____

_____ (the bad habit). I call in the healing Masters and guides to assist me. I call forth the energy of the universe to assist me.

I go to the past and remove all feelings, thoughts, addictions, be released now!

I command that all entities, demons, energies which assist the habit to continue, be gone!!!

Storytime:

Katherine Beck taught, "There is not any such thing as a bad habit, because there really isn't anything that is 'bad' per se, energetically. They are just choices."

God put everything on Earth for our use and to teach our souls.

God is Love, Love is all God is. God created perfection in our bodies.

Our body is created with God's Love.

Imperfection, or lack of unconditional Love, starts at conception, with the thoughts of our parents. Their thoughts, if they stray from unconditional Love, create changes within our cellular matrix. My thoughts then stray from the Love that I am.

God gave me intelligence to know when to use substances and not use.

Feel in your heart what you should do with the habit.

Is it time to choose Love again?

I use Love to change.

I will Love my body healthy and strong.

Love conquers all.

Storytime:

One day, I met a man who had recently been diagnosed with lung cancer. He was told by his doctor that if he didn't stop smoking, the doctor wouldn't take care of him anymore and told them to get out of his office. He was only 49 years old when he walked into Health & Longevity. He was pretty discouraged and felt a huge lack of Love.

I looked at him intuitively. His general aura was very bright. However, a black blob of energy with tentacles was attached all around his chest. (I call these black blobs 'globtapuses' which create and focus fear).

I called in the Master healers to help remove it, so I could see his heart chakra. His heart chakra appeared gray with holes in the lungs and liver. I told him that I knew he was a good man, but as a young man he had started to smoke in order to be accepted by others. This was due to a lack of self Love.

I told him, "I desire to transfer unconditional Love from heaven to fill and heal your heart, lungs and liver. I'll use toning energy to do it."

I started to sing to his heart with an 'om', followed with an 'ah'. He started to weep, tears streaming down his face, but with a big smile. He could feel his heart for the first time in many years.

I explained to him, what a good man his aura was showing me. He is married, has a young wife and four children. All of his family was encouraging him to stop smoking, but without feeling 'self Love', he couldn't find the courage to stop. Lack of self worth, self- Love was what stopped him from quitting this habit, that was killing him. I looked at him and I said "You're a good man, but sometimes good men have habits that make them sick. I will look into your heart today and remove this habit from your heart."

I continued to fill the black and gray areas of cancer in his lungs, and had moved into his heart, liver and lymph glands associated with the heart and lungs. I further saw negative energy associated with the emotional body, as I looked further into his energy field. I could see emotional traumas had occurred.

He had fought in Iraq during 'Desert Storm'and had seen very difficult situations and this was when he started this habit. Starting to smoke gave him something to do to keep his mind off of these negative situations, which the men could relate to each other and talk about the situation to get the memories off of his mind. Even though starting to smoke bothered him, it helped him deal with his anger. This anchor set the stage to connect smoking to dealing with other emotions as well.

I asked him if he would like to quit smoking. He stated," I've tried to stop smoking a thousand times." I asked again, "Will you stop smoking?" He said, "Of course I will".

When he made this commitment, I did a visualization and regression therapy with him. I took him back to the point where he started to smoke. I saw him gathering with some other military men. They were talked about how they had no control with what was happening around them. When they offered a cigarette, instead of feeling so frustrated, he felt good to be part of a group, part of the discussion, discussing their mutual frustration.

We held the emotion of the behavior visualized. We created a new scenario, where instead of taking a cigarette, he said, "no thank you" when he was offered the cigarette. He never started smoking, never took the first drag off of the first cigarette. At that moment in time, instead of his being angry and frustrated with the war, we changed the details, memories, and passion, with his experiences of the war. We sent Love, peace, and compassion to this experience, and his soul started shining brightly, his heart, lungs, lymph and liver, energetically improved dramatically with changes incorporated into his organs which no longer appeared like he had ever started smoking.

We then moved forward in time with the pathways to creating a new reality and time line, that he never started smoking. We brought him forward in time, space and dimension that all of his life was filled with self -Love and incorporating that he never did start smoking.

We then brought forward the energy and time line of a non-smoking existence. I started toning again (Healing God sounds) singing to his lungs, liver, lymph and his heart and solar plexis chakras, emotional body, mental body, physical body creating new energy within his body, then bringing him forward to this life, his heart, lungs, liver, lymph being perfect with new energy, without ever having smoked.

He started coughing severely, had to go up to the sink and coughed out huge amounts of black sputum and mucus. I started him on a program of herbs to cleanse his lungs and to continue the healing, Today this man is cancer free and is no longer smoking.

TODAY I WILL GO TO A SECLUDED LOCATION TO THINK AND MEDITATE IN NATURE

I will go to a favorite spot for secluded breathing and meditation.
I will go with the intent to clear my thoughts and my energy.
I will go with the intent to heal my body.

When I arrive at the secluded location I will find a place where I can be alone.

I will clear the energy around me, cleared with my intent.

I will feel the energy of the plants, the animals, the insects, the earth, water, air, rocks and become one with them and send them Love.

As I sense their bodies, their energy, and their source of energy, I will ask them permission to share their space and energy.

I will send the plants, the animals, insects, the earth, water, air, and rocks the energy of unconditional love and compassion.

I will focus on that energy and ask if the plants, the animals, the earth, the air, and all the other elements, if they will share their energy with me. Not so much that it depletes them, but just enough from each of them that I feel the energy to help me heal and enter into my body.

As I receive that energy, I will show gratitude and thankfulness in my heart for the energy.

I will take the energy and incorporate it, into my body, wherever I desire to heal.

I will again send love and gratitude to the plants, the animals, the insects, the earth, the air, the water, and all the other elementals and the universe for giving me love and energy.

Storytime:

When we were in Peru two years ago, one of the women who participated on the trip, had arrived very sick and tired. She seemed put off and unhappy, uable to get up, move around and enjoy the trip.

The flight to Peru had been very hard on her system. She was having trouble adjusting to the altitude. She would sit in the van struggling to breathe, while we would hike and experience the various spiritual locations.

It was my desire for everyone to enjoy the trip and gain energy and knowledge from the spiritual locations.

So I decided to help her and teach her about the plants and the insects, the wind, the air, the earth, the water, the fire energy and all the other elementals.

I told her to put forth love to the plants the animals, the insects, the wind, the air, the earth, fire, water and all the elementals and ask them to help her by giving a small portion of their energy, not enough to harm them, but just enough to help her have energy.

As she did this, she received energy. I told her to have gratitude to all the elements of the Earth for that energy and to thank them.

We were going up to see an area where the ancient Peruvians hiked to Machu Picchu from Cusco. There were beautiful fountains of water coming out from the mountain. The beauty was remarkable. The added energy which we gathered from nature with gratitude and love filled our hearts and our lungs with strength for the hike.

It all felt so good. With kinesiology, I tested if it harmed the elements of the earth. I heard a resounding "no." They love us to love them and they will give us whatever we desire. Since we only ask for a little bit, they can continue to live and flourish and this makes them love us even more.

TODAY I BEGIN HERBAL TREATMENT FOR ARTERITIS AND VASCULITIS FOR 3-6 MONTHS

The inflammation caused by arteritis and vasculitis can cause partial or complete blockage of blood vessels, narrowing of blood vessels, or the weakening of the walls of a blood vessel (known as an aneurysm). Pain from inflammation can be in the extremities, or afflict any organ affected including the brain with new headaches.

The symptoms depend on how extensive the inflammation is and where it occurs in the body. Symptoms of arteritis may follow a pattern:

- First stage – Sinusitis, Bronchial infection, fatigue, malaise, muscle aches, joint pain, headaches, skin rash, fever, weight loss, blood clots, swelling and inflammation or pain of one or more extremity (arms or legs), difficulty breathing. Parasite or fungal infection can bring the virus and/or atypical bacteria into the body.

- Second stage - this is known as the vascular inflammatory stage, which may cause pain in the extremities and joints, arm numbness, blurry or double vision, headaches, or shortness of breath and high Blood Pressure. These symptoms occur because of reduced blood supply to the affected area due to inflammation. Occasionally, the first and second stage symptoms occur together. Definitely demonstrates an infectious cause with additional bugs (Parasites, Virus, Fungus with atypical bacteria and/or virus)

- Third stage - Chronic Hypertension and continuing damage to the blood vessels and hardening of the arteries. Definitely demonstrates an infectious cause with hiding of the viruses, bacteria in the intima lining of the larger blood vessels causing athero-sclerosis and plaque formation. Varicosities occur externally and internally in organs.

Treatment Plan	morning	lunch	dinner	bed

- On an empty stomach, internal enzymes dissolve the clots and fibrin plaques

Nattokinase 100mg	1 capsules			1 capsules

Reduces plaque and dissolves fibrin clots

Treatment Plan (continued)	morning	lunch	dinner	bed
Serrapeptase 20,000 units	1 capsules		1 capsules	1 capsules

Dissolves internal scar tissue and reduces scarring from arteritis/ vasculitis

#3 Bactrex or BactoEx	2 capsules		2 capsules	2 capsules

Kills bad bacteria

#4 FungDx or PhungEx	2 capsules		2 capsules	2 capsules

rids the body of fungus and yeast

#5 Stabilizer or ViruEx	1 capsules		1 capsules	1 capsules

rids the DNA and cells of abnormal virus and atypical bacteria
With food take the following:

Very Berry solaray 450 mg 1 capsules Breakfast 1 cap Dinner, rids body of atypical bacteria and virus			
Grape Seed Extract 100 mg	1 capsules x 3 with each meal,	aids with repair of blood vessels	
Vitamin K-2 200 mcg	1 capsules x 3 with each meal,	aids with repair of blood vessels	
L-Citrulline	750mg	1 capsules x 3 with each meal,	aids with repair of blood vessels
Resveratrol 100-200mg	1 capsule	helps rid body of atypical bacteria and virus.	

aids with repair of blood vessels

Take Magnesium citrate 200mg morning and 400 mg at night for softening the intima of the vessels

Vitamin C with bioflavonoids 500/500 mg morning lunch and dinner

Rutin 500mg twice daily (powerful anti-oxidants which repair blood vessels)

Oral chelators or IV chelation can also be done during this protocol and will help with recovery.

Treat for three-six months	May require longer treatment according to severity of infection.

TODAY I START A PATHOGEN PURGE

I will begin a protocol to get rid of disease causing pathogens such as viruses, bacteria, atypical bacteria such as mycoplasma, chlamydia, Clostridia dificil, fungus (all kinds) and microscopic parasites. Pathogens such as the these, create a bio-film. This bio-film supports the survival of the pathogens and thwarts the efforts of our immune system. This "goo" shields them from the white blood cells and the parasites excrete toxic waste products, that further weakens the immune system. In order to break down this toxic waste and bio-film, our body needs the help of enzymes to break down the bio-film and remove the toxins to begin the process of eliminating the pathogens.

Dr. Jack Tips helped perfect the way to remove this biofilm using Systemic Formulas.

Today I will begin a protocol to get rid of pathogens which have created bio-film and toxins within my body.

This is a basic Bio-film pathogen purge from Systemic formulas and Inno-Vita. It will take three – twelve cycles or months to complete. Test with kinesiology with your health care provider.

The following is a program from Systemic Formulas***

Empty Stomach	Morning	Lunch	Dinner	Bed	Qty.	Cost
VIVI anti-viral	1 capsules		1 capsule	1 capsule	2	$56.00
Cat's A Tonic	½ dropper		½ dropper	½ dropper	1	$42.00
#3 Bactrex	1 capsule		1 capsule	1 capsule	1	$27.00
ATAK	1 capsule		1 capsule	1 capsule	1	$26.00
#4 FungDx	1 capsule		1 capsule	1 capsule	1	$27.00
MELA	1 capsule		1 capsule	1 capsule	1	$52.00
Gold	1 capsule		1 capsule	1 capsule	1	$32.00
ENZEE	1 capsule		1 capsule	1 capsule	1	$48.00

***Contact your Health professional for questions when starting a nutritional program.

The following is a program from Inno-Vita***

Empty Stomach	Morning	Lunch	Dinner	Bed	Qty.	Cost
ViruEx anti-viral	1 capsules		1 capsule	1 capsule	1	$26.00
Ser-culate	1 capsules		1 capsule	½ dropper	1	$26.00
BactoEx	1 capsules		1 capsule	1 capsule	1	$26.00
Xpleen	1 capsule		1 capsule	1 capsule	1	$25.00
PhungDx	1 capsules		1 capsule	1 capsule	1	$27.00
Redoccin	1 capsules		1 capsule	1 capsule	1	$57.00
Kidney Klear	1 capsule		1 capsule	1 capsule	1	$28.00
Integra-Cell	1 scoop				1	$52.00
Micro-Site	1 capsule		1 capsule	1 capsule	1	$31.00

***Contact your Health professional for questions when starting a nutritional program

Remember to increase water intake and keep elimination pathways open, liver, digestive tract, lymph, spleen and kidneys. This protocol will help when you have bio-film with small abscesses.

Story time:

A woman came to our store with chronic abscesses and infections, which had plagued her for seven years. Medical doctors had tried every anti-biotic, and still the infection continued with resistance developing.

She agreed to follow the above protocols for twelve months, switching every other month. By the end of the third month, the infection of her skin disappeared. She asked if she could stop, but the kinesiology indicated the infection was still present in her organs, so we continued.

After a year of treatment, we discontinued, and three years later, she is still infection free!

TODAY I BEGIN A SIMPLE FUNGAL/ YEAST CLEANSE FOR 3 MONTHS

Cleaning and removing fungus/yeast is essential for slowing the body's deterioration. If I look in my fridge at the food that is older, I find fungus growing on the food. My body is very similar. If I haven't been using my body appropriately, by eating too many sugars, too many breads or starches, I find fungus/yeast growing in my body. Yes, pasta is a starch.

Today I will reduce the sugars being taken into my body and start a fungal/yeast cleanse. My cravings for sugar are due to the fungus/ yeast in my body. Today I command that yeast/fungus to be removed from my body, and I will stop feeding the fungus/yeast.

Today I take back control of my body. This body is a Temple of love. I vibrate in love. Fungus vibrates in fear, lack and cravings. Fungus also makes me feel alone, without strength, foggy headed and not in control. I'm just feeling I need to be around others with fungus, so that I can eat sugar with them and provide a feast for the fungus.

Today I do a simple fungal/yeast cleanse and I take back my life.

I will take the following till gone to remove fungus from my body.

1st month

Provermifuge (PHP)	2 capsules		2 capsules	2 capsules	1	$29.99
Yeast Cleanse (Solaray)	2 capsules		2 capsules	2 capsules	1	$28.99
Rascal (Kroeger Herbs)	1 caps		1 capsule	1 capsule	1	$12.99
Oregano Caps (LA naturals)	1 caps		1 capsule	1 capsule	1	$19.99
With food	Take the	Following				
Multidophilus-12	1 capsule	1 capsule	1 capsule		1	$28.99
Pumpkin Seed oil	2 capsules		2 capsules		1	$13.99

After the above is gone, I will take the following till gone: 2nd month

#4 FungDx	1 caps	1 capsule	1 capsule	1 capsule	2	($27) $54.00
Ls Liver Stabilizer	2 capsules				1	$23.00
Lb Liver/Gall		2 capsules			1	($18
Ps Pancreas Stabilizer			2 capsules		1	$22.00
L Liver Builder				2 capsules	1	$18.00

After the above is gone, I will take the following till gone:

PhungDx	1 caps	1 capsule	1 capsule	1 capsule	2	($27) $54.00
Livergy	2 capsules				1	$28.00
Gall-Astic		2 capsules			1	$24
Pancreos			2 capsules		1	$27.00
ToxEx				2 capsules	1	$31.00

If this protochol keeps coming up, a deep seated fungal infection is present or sugars may be too abundant in the diet. It took the Author of this book, four years to get the fungus/yeast under control. I continue to take anti-fungals when ever I attend weddings, funerals, Birthday parties due to the sugars available.

Life is sweet!!! So today, I rid my body of fungal/yeast.

TODAY I WILL SAY KIND
WORDS TO MYSELF

Today I will be nice, I treat myself with respect, and I love myself. Today is the first day of the rest of my life. My life will be full of bliss and joy and happiness because I love myself and I say kind words to myself.

Words and thoughts are things. I listen to the words in my ears and incorporate them into my brain, my cells, my organs and my body. My synapses incorporate them into my neural functions and pathways, and the more I say the words or listen to the thoughts, the deeper the connections become.

Today I will incorporate kind words into my thoughts and thought forms.

Storytime:

I can remember waking up feeling really great about myself. Then I had someone say something to me which made me feel badly about myself. I started thinking what a bad person I was, especially that this person, who loved me, would say something, that made me think what a bad person I was.

Why would she say that? What was I doing that caused her to say that? Am I really that bad of a person?

These thoughts and words started incorporating into my psyche. What about this is totally wrong?

Soon I found myself grumbling, scuffing my feet on the floor, shoulder's shrugging, back hurting, head pain, neck stiffness, every pain in the book coming upon me quickly and easily overcoming my strength.

I was allowing these words to affect my body and make me feel unworthy, in pain, and disgusted with myself.

Then I recognized what I was doing. I was punishing myself, blaming myself, for an incorrect perception, a misperceived comment, coming from another individual.

"Wait a minute," I said to myself. "I'm a very good person, loving, giving, healing, encouraging. Every day I wake up and pray for others and have a desire to serve others."

"I am a kind person. I am someone I wish I had for a friend. I think kind thoughts about myself."

And all of a sudden all my pain went away, all my negative thoughts, went away.

It's amazing how we incorporate our thoughts into our body.

From God, at conception, I am perfect.

I enter the world in unconditional Love.

I am perfection manifest into this life.

I create my perception.

I Love myself.

I am in Love with myself

Today I will say kind things to myself.

TODAY I PRAY FOR HELP.

Today I will say a prayer, whether out loud, or in my heart, to have the people, a person, or entities of light, come into my space to help me with my health or other problems.

Prayer is a powerful modality for getting answers. Prayer comes from my soul.

Prayer is a communication with source energy and the universe.

Prayer puts me in contact with the angels and beings of light and the Masters of healing.

Prayer keeps me humble to receive answers.

Prayer opens space to receive love, light, and communication from the heavens.

Prayer touches the lives of those who will help me.

Prayer sets in motion the emotions of the higher consciousness.

Prayer will draw to me my healing and those who will help me heal.

Prayer gathers the source energy to help me heal.

Prayer brings unconditional love and compassion into my life.

Prayer blesses my life and the lives of those who I love.

Prayer helps me to understand what I should do and where I should go, and who I should be with.

Prayer creates a positive vortex of energy for me to make contact with the universe.

I am grateful for prayer and its influence in my life.

Today I will pray for help.

Storytime:

About four years ago Vicki and I had a very strong impression, both of us at the same moment, that we were supposed to move to North Carolina. This impression was so strong we put the house up for sale and made plans with a realtor to buy a house in North Carolina.

I always like to visit herbal stores when I travel so that I can help people wherever I go. We looked on the computer and found an herb store in North Carolina in Charlotte. I called the owner and made arrangements to do medical intuitive readings on a particular day.

The owner of the store was having financial difficulties keeping the store open and this was a store which I chose to come to. She had lined up 40 clients for me to see and do medical intuitive readings and healings.

When we arrived at the store, people were already waiting in anticipation of our visit and healings.

The first seven people had issues with parasites and fungus, which are common medical concerns. When the eighth person came in, I knew she was special. Her entire right side was sagging, her arm on the right side useless and she was dragging her right leg. Her face was drooping and immediately I felt and heard the number three -- that she had had a stroke at the age of three years old. When I said this to her, she stated that she had had three strokes at the age of three. Sickle cell anemia, had caused her to have a sickle cell crisis at the age of three and she ended up in the hospital with three complicated strokes leaving her paralyzed on her right side.

She said to me, "You have come to heal me. I prayed to be healed and you have come." The strength of her words actually gave me strength but also stunned me with her faith. She stated, "I was praying for help, I don't want to stay paralyzed my entire life." She knew someone was coming. She knew God was sending her someone to help her heal.

I felt very inadequate. I knew what she wanted and desired. I felt her faith and with that faith and belief, it gave me strength to do something I have just learned the previous week. Intuitively, I closed my eyes and I visualized her face, the muscles and the nerves in the tissues, the blood vessels being perfect. Perfection within the tissues, bones and cartilage. I visualized the connections to her nervous system being perfect and all of the body straightening and being perfected.

I started to hear sounds of amazement from the eight people present in the room. I opened my eyes to see a beautiful 28-year-old black woman standing, up right and perfect in front of me.

Her face no longer drooped. Instead of slouching over on a cane, she stood up right, straight, and strong.

I started to cry, knowing her prayer had been answered. I know it wasn't me who delivered the healing. It was her prayers and her faith. To this day, I am so grateful to be able to be a part of that experience.

TODAY I WILL ENCOURAGE
OTHERS TO HEAL

Today I say encouraging words, I will set an example for myself and others to heal.

I am an example of healing.

I project the energy of healing and being healed.

I am positive and encouraging to others today.

I tell stories of healing and of miracles.

If I don't have any stories of healing and miracles today, I will create a miracle.

I will talk positively, with faith and encourage miracles.

I remember the experiences of healing in my life.

I will call and encourage a friend.

Today, I will encourage others to heal, which will help me heal.

Storytime:

Four years ago when Vicki and I traveled to Charlotte, North Carolina after visiting an herbal store and seeing miraculous healings occur, we decided to look on the computer to choose a church to attend as it was Sunday. The church we were drawn to was the Unity Church of Charlotte. We found the address and proceeded to drive to the church. When we arrived, we entered in and found a seat. The minister was very grateful to see us and shook our hands.. We sat down and listened to the sermon, which on that day was about how the unity Church had begun.

The minister began a story of healing. In the 1800s a woman had consumption (tuberculosis), and was told by her physician she was going to die. She was only in her 20s. She desired to live. She remembered the stories of the healings that Jesus had done in the New Testament.

She prayed to be healed and it came to her to visualize Jesus sitting in a chair in front of her, healing her, making her perfect.

So each day she sat down in the chair and put another chair in front of her and visualized Jesus healing her body, healing her soul, healing her completely and perfectly.

Every day her health improved.

Her husband, who had been run over by a wagon, and was troubled with pain, crippled in his hip and leg, watched as his wife, instead of dying of consumption, began to improve and to heal.

After a time she was completely healed of the tuberculosis through her visualization and faith.

Her husband, an atheist, who did not believe in any higher being or purpose, asked his wife how she had done this. She related to him that she visualized Jesus healing her every day and making her body perfect and drawing out the infection of consumption from her.

Her husband had seen the miracle but was still in disbelief. He asked if she thought he could do the same, even though he didn't believe. She told him, yes, even though there was no faith or belief, she felt that if he would visualize and try to see Jesus and ask for the help that he would be healed. She would help him and pray for him and his healing.

Her husband would sit in a chair with another chair in front of him and each day he would pray and visualize for his healing even though he didn't believe. His actions however true for the forces of heaven and source energy, each day he improved until one day he felt a loud noise in his hip. His hip popped into place and he stood up and walked without his cane. Now, I don't know that I've told this story precisely, but even the atheist husband was healed through his efforts to heal. Through the encouragement of his wife and her example he was able to heal himself.

I was so impressed by this story I felt the need to get up and teach breathing to heal and help the congregation. The minister asked for visitors to get up and tell something about themselves, so Vicki, encouraged by this story, took up courage, walked up and started to tell about how we had come to North Carolina to move there, and buy a house. She told the story of the healing the previous day at the herbal store. She told how we believed in faith, the healing and encouragement of others. She then said, that I had wanted to teach them about breathing.

I went in front of the congregation and taught them a method of breathing that Jesus had taught me.

The minister was very grateful and invited us to stay for lunch.

In the rear of the building, a woman in a wheelchair had been taking notes during the entire meeting. As we walked down the aisle to leave, she grabbed my hand, and said, "I prayed and you have come to heal me". As I looked at her, I saw her feet which were both infected. Her toes, were covered with sores, pustules, wounds and gangrene. Several of the toes looked as if they were going to fall off. I felt she had severe diabetes and the wounds in her feet were due to her diabetes being out of control for many years.

She stated, "The surgeons want to remove my feet, and I've been praying to be healed. You are the answer to my prayers". Again, I felt so inadequate, so lacking in the power she desired. However, I was encouraged by what had happened the previous day to the woman with sickle cell anemia, who had three strokes at the age of three, who had been healed. I had nothing to lose by assisting this woman.

I asked her, "Do you have the faith to be healed?" She emphatically answered, "Yes"

I closed my eyes, as I held her hand, and I told her to have faith in Jesus and I visualized the circulation to her feet being perfect, the tissues, bones and sinews of her feet, the tissues repairing and being perfect. Again, the people surrounding us, started to murmur and gasp as her feet healed before our eyes.

I opened my eyes to see her feet perfected, I told her to stand up and give the glory to God. She started to walk, without her wheelchair. As we walked, she hugged me and told me how grateful she was for me being an answer to her prayers, and encouraging her faith through our description of what had happened the previous day. The minister of the church, needless to say, stated, "we would love to have you as a permanent part of our congregation".

After the healings in North Carolina, we flew back home, the desire and the need to move to Charlotte went away. Our house never sold, and we are still in St. George. I know the feeling to go to North Carolina was not to move there, but to assist and encourage others to heal.

Today I encourage others to heal and by doing so, I will be healed.

TONIGHT I WILL ASK TO HAVE A DREAM OR AN ANSWER TO MY HEALTH PROBLEMS

Tonight as I lie down to bed, I will ask a question, and have faith to have that answered my dreams.

As I sleep, beings of light, the Angels, the fairies, the elementals-- who all vibrate in unconditional Love, will bring me the answers to that question.

I will have a dream, a prompting, a name, an answer, come to me and I will remember the answer.

I will wake up and write down the answer.

I will write down the details of the dream or the name I receive.

I will act on the answer I receive.

Storytime:

Five years ago a man with stage IV colon cancer prayed the night before for an answer, because he desired to be healed. The surgeons were going to do an extensive surgery removing; remove the colon, his lymph nodes and part of his bladder and prostate to remove what cancer they could. They had given him very little hope of a cure or even a chance to have a normal life after the surgery.

Being spiritual, he headed to the Temple in St. George to pray. In the temple as he prayed, the name Scott Werner-- came to his mind. A man very near to him was also praying, and his prayer ended about the same time. He was prompted to ask the other man if he knew a Scott Werner. He was delighted to tell him that yes, he had been healed from heart disease, and had done chelation therapy with a Dr. Scott Werner up in Cedar City, Utah. Scott Werner had moved to St. George five years ago. He then gave the address to the person with the colon cancer.

He stated that he was now in St. George Utah doing herbal work and intuitive healing.

Within hours, this man was at our office asking for an intuitive reading. I discussed with him stories of faith, stories of healing, encouraging his faith. I told him that his faith, his desires, his visualization of his body perfecting, with the assistance of the herbs would help him to heal.

Yesterday, this same man came to my office. He stated that he had just had a five-year checkup and he was still cancer free.

He prayed, he asked, he desired, he had faith to act, and the universe gave him his answer and he was healed.

TODAY I DO ANOTHER
PARASITE CLEANSE.

I love my body, and I'm removing parasites from my body, which are keeping me from healing.

Parasites come in many forms.

There are large segmented parasites. Flat and round parasites. Long and skinny parasites. Cellular or microscopic parasites.

Parasites can come in the other forms, resembling spirochetes, fungus, molds, spores, bacteria and viruses

They are called parasites because they suck out my life force, they live off my organs, tissues, and cause disease.

Today I start another parasite cleanse.

Storytime:

Over the past 25 years, I have done parasite cleanses. I was told to do them every three months for the rest of my life. To keep cancer from recurring. I have been faithful in doing that. The only time I was unable to do parasite cleanses was when the federal government didn't allow me to, and during that time, cancer recurred my right upper arm. It was very painful. I could not even sleep on it. It felt like it had grown into the ball joints and bone. I lost weight rapidly, the food being given me was either rotted or had no nutritional value. It was a sad time in my life.

Jesus appeared to me and said, "Do you want to get out of here? If you stay in here you will die, but if you choose to get out, you will have to agree to make a plea bargain with the prosecuting attorney." "You will have to let go of your wanting to be right, your fight for a cause, and even though you didn't do anything wrong, you will have to admit to one count of medical insurance fraud." "They also want you to give up your medical license for the rest of your life and never practice medicine in the United States of America again. They will also want you to pay the fines, interest, penalties, and fees to the one count of insurance fraud." I told Jesus "I will do it."

The next day I called my wife on the phone and talked to her about what I had decided to do. Vicki was elated for I had been away far too long and she knew if I didn't get home, I would die. The rest is history, and I am a free man, and I am again free of cancer. I was able to come home, and start another parasite cleanse. Getting rid of parasites in our life and in our body is very important. I choose to live.

Today I will start another parasite cleanse.

Provermafuge PHP	3 capsules		3 capsules	3 capsules	1	$29.99
Rascal Kroeger Herbs	2 capsules		2 capsules	2 capsules	1	$12.99
Pumpkinseed oil	2 capsules		2 capsules	2 capsules	1	$13.99
CLNZ chelator Systemic Formulas				2 capsules	1	$24.00

Today I will find joy in my life

Joy is something that makes us happy.

   Joy makes life worth living.

   Joy is the juice that flows through our body and helps us rejoice that our life.

   Joy is a state of Bliss.

   Joy brings happiness to our lives.

   Joy helps us heal.

   Joy releases negative thoughts and emotions

   Joy and pain cannot exist in the same space

   Storytime:

   Several years back, a woman who could find no joy in her life came to see me.

   Her life was full of drudgery, obligations, children who were demanding, a husband who was never satisfied, and constant cleaning up the messes of others.

   She wanted to feel Joy. She wanted to be made whole. She had called upon her religious beliefs to heal, without results. She was now ready to move on and heal. Her body was worn out, her mind full of negative thought forms. She was constantly getting ill and her old belief system was exhausted.

   I asked her, "Do you have any joy in your life?" She stated that with all her obligations and beliefs, the joy was out of her life. The religion had become toxic, the requirements--burdens and there was no joy even in attending her church.

   Intuitively, I knew she had to be released from her false beliefs, the drudgery, thoughts of this going on for eternity.

   I told her that she would receive an answer by praying. I told her that she would have Joy return to her life in following the feelings of her heart.

She went home and prayed and found the answers to her prayers. She started following her heart. She started making changes in her life that were against her religion, her family, and her tribe. She eventually moved away to another country and started a whole new life. When I asked her about it, she stated, "I now have joy in my life".

TODAY I FACE MY FEARS

Today, I face my fears by naming them and asking the universe to help me remove them.

What are my fears?

A fear of heights or water or being alone?

A fear of people, animals, dogs or cats?

I will write down, my biggest fear in this moment.

I desire to think about my life without the fear.

Fear holds power over me, and keeps me from progressing.

Fear keeps me from vibrating in faith.

Fear is the opposite of faith.

Fear blocks progression and evolution.

Fear keeps me from opening my heart to loving, satisfying relationships.

Fear keeps me where I am at, rather than being where I would like to be.

Fear is smothering, preventing me from being with higher minded people, I would love to be with.

Fear is restricting, stopping me from being who I want to be and keeping me from healing my body.

Today I conquer the fear within me. What I conquer today, no longer holds me back.

Today, I face my fear, and conquer it with faith in myself and in God.

Storytime:

While I was on Maui, in the Hawaiian islands, I faced several of my fears. One of my greatest, is fear of heights. Every time I go up in a tall building or I'm in an airplane, or on top of a mountain, my stomach gets rigid and I get severe digestive aches and pains. I fear I'm going to jump off or be pushed off when I get close to the edge.

I woke up today (written on the day I was in Maui) and was told to go to the top of the Haleakala volcano. I really didn't want to go.

(and was making excuses to not face my fear). But the mountain was the clearest I'd seen it, since being on the island, and I knew it was my time to go.

As I drove up, it was a gorgeous day and was just starting to become light in the eastern sky. The curves became more tight, pronounced and I couldn't see off to the side. It seemed like there was a drop-off and my stomach started feeling that pain that I get, with my fear of heights. I entered the national Park and pulled off to the visitor center to see how much further I had to go. My soul knew I had to go to the top.

I got back on the road, which became even more narrow and torturous. There were no guard rails. Each time I would steer around the curve, it seemed like I was driving off the edge. My nerves felt frazzled. As I climbed the volcano I knew this was going to be a different sort of story. A de ja vu, I had climbed this volcano on foot in another existence.

Clouds appeared and it started raining upon the truck. The road became slippery and even more narrow. The rain turned into a snow storm, right there in Hawaii, As I approached the top a gale force wind blowing all around me, almost moving the truck off the side of the road.

Luckily there was parking at the top and I was the only one at the top of the volcano in this moment. I climbed the stairs to a small building that had been built on top of the peak of the volcano. I looked around and I felt I should walk to the other side where there was also a rising portion of the volcano.

As I stood on the peak, and the wind surged, I felt as though I'd be blown off the cliff, down into the clouds below, I felt as if I was going to be carried off into the air, off the side of the cliff. A voice inside of me whispered, "Ground yourself to the earth, into the magma ". I again, went into fear of flying off. Again the voice whispered, "Ground yourself into the magma of the earth". The thought that came to me was , that in a past life, I had actually jumped into the volcano when it was an active volcano with red-hot molten magma.

I grounded myself into the earth, asking for God to give me strength. As I grounded myself, my fear disappeared and there was a feeling of peace. The wind slowed to just the slight breeze against my face. The rain stopped, clouds disappeared, and the sun appeared, which gave me a glimpse of the beauty surrounding me ,what was actually there. It was beautiful as now I could see the ocean. I could see the little valleys and rainbows with their multicolored beauty. There even appeared a silver rainbow, I could see the beauty of this creation. I felt the fear leave my body, and in it's place, entered faith.

Next I heard a voice saying, "You've overcome this fear, and now it's time to confront your next fear." The voice continued and predicted, " Today you will be swimming with whales and dolphins in the deep blue ocean." Immediately, the fear of drowning in the ocean came streaming in to me. I saw myself in a past life, swimming between Maui and Lanai, in the center of the deep blue, with dolphins and whales swimming around me. I had drowned.

Driving down the volcano I received a phone call. It's Anne Musellman , who is an angel, who guided me on my whole journey on Maui. She stated, "There is a sail boat, with Captain Pierre, which is going out into the ocean to be with the whales and dolphins." Anne said, "I have to work all day, but I want you to go in my place."

I thanked her for the opportunity to go. I was very excited, but I knew I would have to face my other fear. She said that we would be swimming outside of the boat and be able to do many things which many whale watchers are unable to do. Again, in the pit of my stomach, my fear of the 'big blue' started to show it's ugly face.

I arrived on the west coast, small town of Lahaina, Maui, found a side street to park, and waded off the shore to the waiting sail boat.

As we went out on the boat, it occurred to me that this was where I had been 500 years ago in a competitive swim between Maui and Lanai. I had made it half way and had drowned. One of the women on the boat seemed so familiar and yet I have never met her before, in this lifetime. We made an instant connection.

As we talked on the boat I came to see this was my partner in a lifetime many years past. She had watched me drown and was extremely sad for my loss.

We started seeing whales, tails at first, and then when they were breaching the water with their entire bodies, and finally, a whole family coming closer to the boat. I was scared, I sat on the edge with my snorkel mask on waiting, waiting, waiting. The fear in me was rising. I was terrified. I did not desire to even get in the water. I asked myself? Do I jump in with the possibility of drowning?

I sat for about five minutes on the side of the boat trying to decide whether I was going to jump in, the fear in me building. From behind me I heard the words, "Well, what are you waiting for?"

I jumped off the side of the boat and my whole body went rigid, arms and legs paralyzed, I sank down into the water, I could feel my spine spasming. Then, everything inside of me just hurting, with my lungs longing for air. I realized, "I couldn't breathe."

My first thought was, "I'm going to drown again."

My second thought, "I promised Vicki, I would come home."

All of a sudden I felt something pushed me from underneath my buttocks. The pressure increased, and I felt myself going up fast. A smaller whale, probably only 1500 lbs, pushed me up, up, up, right out of the water. I was frightened, but got some air. I started paddling towards the boat, but Pierre yelled, "Don't splash, you'll attract the sharks." So I swam very quietly and carefully over to the ladder of the boat. I climbed up out of the water and my whole body was in pain.

I set down inside the boat. I noticed everyone was having a great time watching the whales. I said to myself I need to get back in the water. I didn't die. I needed to face this fear. So I stood on the front end of the boat and jumped into the deep blue, without fear.

I was amazed at how easily I swam in the water, like I was one of the dolphins. My back released the tension, muscles felt strong.

What was very interesting about this was how the woman who was a partner in a past life kept telling me, when I went down into the water the first time, that she was very afraid I was going to drown. She was ready to jump in and save me. She was so grateful when I breached out of the water. She had to be there to see me live, not drown, so that we could complete and release the cycle of a past lifetime.

TODAY I START AN INTENSE ANTIVIRAL HOMEOPATHIC FOR THE NEXT SIX MONTHS

Viruses usually enter into the system due to negative emotions toward the self.

The emotions of guilt, shame, blame, and humiliation are very powerfulforces for allowing viruses into my cells.

Viruses are present on everything I touch, smell, breathe and ingest.

My immune system will identify and tag all viruses in my system.

Homeopathic's are an excellent remedy to help my system identify and expel virus from my cells.

I will pop all viruses in my body like popcorn and my immune system will act like little Pac men eating the virus quickly and easily expelling them from my body.

Today I rid my body of virus.

Storytime:

In 1998, a young man, came to my office in search for answers. He was 24 years old and appeared like a skeleton in front of me. Instantly, my intuition told me, he had a retro virus which was causing the auto immune disorder known commonly as AIDs.

He asked me if I could help him. My intuition said yes. Homeopathic's tested intuitively the best, but making a homeopathic from his blood and urine, tested the very best.

What are homeopathic remedies? The founding of homeopathy came into being with the teachings and writings of Dr. Samuel Hahnemann (1755-1843 CE), who was disillusioned with such common medical practices of the day as purging, bloodletting, and the use of toxic chemicals including heavy metal such as mercury for treatment of common maladies. Many physicians were using mercury as a treatment for scarlet fever, typhoid, cholera and yellow fever. The cures were worse than the maladies, the patients would develop 'Mad Hatters disease'.

Dr. Hahnemann 's research into "cures with the idea of similars or likes being cured by likes" is the main principle of homeopathy. Herbs which produced the same symptoms of the disease tended to help cure the disease. Homeopathic Medical schools became very popular in the late 1800s but in the 1920s many of the schools closed under the influence of the American Medical Association.

This young man with AIDS, who had an "incurable viral infection", began a regime of homeopathic medication made from his blood and urine. A 30 X. dilution was used first, with the first 42 day cycle. (42 days or six weeks is the amount of time for cells to divide and make daughter cells). After the 42 days a new 30 X. dilution of his blood and urine was made into a homeopathic and restarted. I was told by Spirit that 10 cycles of 42 days each would be necessary for his body.

We also started him on a raw food diet which consisted of eating fresh organic fruits and vegetables and raw meats especially bison and organic beef. One year later rather than looking like a skeleton, this young man looked like a powerful bodybuilder. His blood work showed me, he no longer had virus or antibodies to the virus in his blood.

This remarkable healing occurred because he was persistent and believed and took his homeopathic as prescribed. He also consumed live food into his system in its natural state with all the enzymes and nutrition present in the food. This is an excellent example of how the body can cure itself when given the correct information and nutrition.

TODAY I WILL EAR CANDLE.

Today I will go to an herb store and purchase 16 ear candles, eight (8) for each ear.

I will learn how to use the ear candles by reading the instructions

Before I light the candle, I will set my intention, to clear negative energy which is stored in my ears, in the occipital lobe of my brain and in the throat chakra

I will light the candle with a match, will have a partner or friend assist me.

I will ear candle each ear today.

I will do this twice a week for four weeks.

Storytime:

About 13 years ago, I had a very powerful men come to me to be healed. This man had fought in the war of Vietnam. He didn't know how many people he had killed. He knew it was at least several hundreds.

His right ear had been damaged with the explosions of gunfire. He asked me if his hearing could be restored.

My intuition told me he needed to use ear candling. I had never heard of ear candling . The herbalist working in the herb shop new exactly the science behind ear candling. He proceeded to tell the history behind ear candling and the energetics behind ear candling. I tested that 16 total candling of each ear or 32 candlings would do the job. We ordered in the ear candles and started treatment.

After eight ear candling 's of his ears, his hearing started to return. A side effect of the ear candling was that negative energies also left his body and system. His mood improved, his attitude toward life and his family improved. He began to forgive himself for what he had done in the war and since the war.

When I asked the herbalist about these positive side effects, he stated that the candles were creating light vortices, drawing out the negative energies within his mind, ears and his energy system. The ear candles were not only clearing physical impairments to his hearing but also the energetic impairments from the killing.

When this client completed the ear candling, his hearing was totally restored to his right ear and the left ear had also made remarkable improvements. His chronic fatigue from all the emotional blame, guilt, and shame from what happened in the war had disappeared.

Ear Candling Instructions

Have a bowl of water close at hand, scissors, matches (or a lighter), a toothpick, and a paper plate, or metal pie tin.

1. Place the subject in a *comfortable position on their side.*
2. Cut a dime-size hole in the paper plate, or pie tin, (This will serve to catch any wax, should some drip from the outside of the candle).
3. Insert the candle through the hole in the plate. Light the large end of the candle, and place the small end firmly seated in the ear canal. If smoke is escaping from the small end, please seat the candle again.

During the process, please hold the candle at a slight angle from perpendicular (at least 20 degrees).

This will keep any melting wax that runs down the inside of the candle from depositing in the ear. Any melting wax will harden before it reaches the tip. This will also slow the small end of the candle from becoming stopped with wax, and residue, during the procedure, providing maximum benefit.

4. After the first 2 minutes, remove the candle from the ear, and clean out the tip with a toothpick. This will keep smoke flowing into the ear canal.

Note: if it is more comfortable, you may hold the candle in a straight up and down position.

5. Remove the candle from the ear about every 3 minutes. Check to see that the tip is open, and trim off the burned portion of the candle into the bowl of water with a sharp pair of scissors. Do not trim away so much that the flame is extinguished. (This will provide maximum injection of the smoke throughout the process.)
6. Let the candle burn down to no closer than 3" from the end. Extinguish the burning end in the bowl of water, and dispose of it in a safe manner.

The session is complete, unless you want to candle the other ear. If so, repeat all steps.

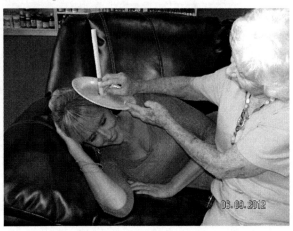

Notes:

A very small amount of ash may fall from the candle during the process. The amount will be negligible, and should not be a cause for concern.

Always keep the flame end up, and the tip down. An ear candle burned with the flame end down will consume in an extremely short time, and is a fire hazard.

TODAY, I WILL HAVE A REFLEXOLOGY TREATMENT OF MY FEET

Today I will find a reflexologist. I know there are three of this healing modality in the book. But I have found this to be very beneficial.

I will ask my herbalist, holistic physician, or naturo path if they know a good reflexologist.

I will schedule an appointment and keep the appointment.

Storytime:

16 years ago, we started doing footbath treatments to detox the feet. During this same time after the detox treatments, we would rub down the feet with olive oil, an ancient ritual.

About the same time, a young woman started doing massage therapy in at the Total Health Center. This young woman knew how to do reflexology treatments. She performed the treatment on my own feet, which assisted with my circulation and health.

We decided to have her teach a reflexology course at the Total Health Center.

20 people showed up for the class. As Fawn taught the class, we all performed reflexology on each other. It was an excellent experience and taught us all the health benefits of reflexology. We also learned the different areas of the foot, which represented the different organs of the body and systems. The rubbing of feet, is very helpful for the circulation and vitality of the organs. It is also very helpful for fatigue and exhaustion of the body systems. Most nights Vicki and I take turns rubbing each other's feet helping each others vitality, organs and sleep.

TODAY I GET ORGANIZED AND CREATE THE UNIVERSE I DESIRE.

Today I organize my life and begin to be where I desire to be. Organization of my life is very or important. It helps me accomplish what I desire.

I wake up with energy each day.

I Accomplish what I desire each day.

Creation requires intent, energy and organization.

Where am I expending my energy?

Am I expending my energy on those things I desire or am I spinning my wheels wondering what I am doing?

Sometime today-- right now would be best --I sit down and organize the rest of my life.

I will get a noteboo, and write down my thoughts and goals in this moment.

Here are some ideas:

I am younger, stronger, healthier, and more beautiful every day.

I receive equal or better exchange for my time and energy.

Money flows to me easily and abundantly.

As my energy expands into the universe I attract people who will help me get what I desire and I will help them get what they desire.

I awake refreshed and ready to greet my day with enthusiasm.

Storytime:

About a year ago, I had a client who didn't know who she was or where she was going. Every day she had a routine in which she worked very hard, but was seeing very few results. This left her empty and un-accomplished inside. She was in a dead-end relationship with someone who was selfish, constantly cheating on her, and giving her venereal disease . At her job, everyone was taking advantage of her and taking away her ability to make money. Spirit told me to sit down and write down her desires with her.

Paper is made from wood, word is made from trees, and trees solidify our thoughts and our desires (goals) planting our desires firmly in the earth. We sat down and talked about writing these manifestations down on paper. Then we wrote them down. She got a big piece of paper and in big bold marking pens wrote them down. Then we hung these desires up, these manifestations, where she could read them every day with emotion,

When manifesting, we write down our desires as if we already accomplished them. In other words, it's not what we need or want (which shows lack), we tell the universe who we are and what we desire, then allow the universe to take care of us. When we desire health, "I am healthy." When we desire wealth, "I am wealthy." When we desire a perfect relationship, "I am a perfect partner." The universe picks up on our intent and thoughts and gives us what we desire. When we write these desires on paper, making the statements every day with the emotion, the energy builds and the universe provides. We are the creators of our own universe

Today I get organized and create the universe I desire

Story time:

Seven years ago, I attended a class which taught about manifesting and writing down our desires on paper.

I wrote ten statements and said them outload, every day with emotion.

All of them, including writing this book, have manifested.

Now it is time to make a new list!

TODAY I CHOOSE TO BE HAPPY

Happiness is a state of being. It is a choice.
Being happy is a state of mind.
I can be happy in any situation. Rich or poor, or anywhere inbetween.
I can be happy in any location.
I can choose to be happy with the people in my life.
I can be happy with myself.
I can be happy for no reason at all.

Storytime:

Last month, when I was in Peru, we had split up into students and teachers. I was a teacher for a person from Santa Fe, NM, and a Principal for a high school in Pennsylvania was my teacher. By the end of the first week, the Principal and I hadn't gotten together yet, so I asked her when she was going to teach me. She stated, "you seem so together, I doubt there is anything I can teach you". I told her to pray about it that night, and ask what she should teach me.

The next morning, she stated, "The Angels came to me, and told me to ask if you are Happy?".

All of a sudden, I heard the words come out of my mouth, "No, I am not happy!". Wow! What was that about? She looked at me in disbelief. Then she started to tell me, "Happiness is a choice. I can be in the worst situation and still be happy."

Then, it dawned on me. I hadn't been happy for some time. Life had become a burden. I was doing things because of obligation, rather than choosing to do them with happiness. My life was a tragic loss of happiness. Don't get me wrong. I laughed at jokes, movies, conversation, but inside, I was just living by the book (My own thoughts and reality), but not living with happiness and joy as my thought pattern.

The Principal went on to say, "Scott, your guides and angels just want you to be happy, to choose to be happy". "Whenever I am in pain, or get injured, I choose not to feel the pain, so it goes away and I keep playing soccer, because soccer makes me happy." "Do what you do, because it helps you to be happy, and choose to be happy in everything you do."

I was like, yes, I desire to be happy, I felt an energy shift within my body, a good shift which raised my vibration, joy and bliss. Today, I choose to be happy!

TODAY I TAKE CARE OF AND NURTURE MYSELF

Today I will plan an activity, which will nurture my body, allow me to rest or enjoy myself.

Today I will take one hour to just be me

My body will be nurtured today

Today and every day, I will take care of me.

What will help me be a better me? Is it exercise? Is it reading a book? Is it cooking the meal I desire?

Is if clearing out my clutter? Is it taking time to meditate? Is it getting out of a bad relationship?

Is it having sex? Is it planning my future? Is it writing my book? Hmmmm?

Today I take care of and nurture myself.

Storytime:

I woke up three weeks ago with the realization that for seven years, I have needed to write a book.

I had desired to write a book and it had never come to fruition. It was because I was always taking care

of other people in my life and not taking care of my own life.

I knew I had to get away, far away.

My favorite place in the world is Hawaii. The Spirit told me I would need at least 18 days to write a book.

But it couldn't be just any book, it was a book about healing. I had been giving lectures about Taking

Back Your Health. The book I spent seven years planning to write was called, *Manifesting Your Health.*

I had written the first eight chapters and never got beyond that in the last five years.

Why didn't the book get done? Was it because it wasn't time yet? Was it because I have writer's cramp?

Was it because I was uninspired?

Then I suddenly understood. I had not been taking care of 'me'.

I knew it was my destiny to write a book. I knew it had to vibrate in unconditional love.

I knew it had to have information which would help others to heal.

I knew that the book had to be an instrument of love from God and the universe. Sometimes, we listen and nurture ourselves.

I am at the end of my trip to Hawaii. I came to write a book, but mainly, to nurture myself by

completing the book to nurture you.

And now, I am writing the final page of "Take Back Your Health" and it feels good.

I finally nurtured myself and took care of what I had desired to do for many years.

And it feels wonderful. And yes, now, I can rest for a time.

I am one with the universe, the universe is one with me, I and the universe are one.

(Adaptation of Chi Gong statement),